Critical Issues in Educational Leadership Series
Joseph Murphy, Series Editor

School Choice in Urban America: Magnet Schools
and the Pursuit of Equity
CLAIRE SMREKAR and ELLEN GOLDRING

Lessons from High-Performing Hispanic Schools:
Creating Learning Communities
PEDRO REYES, JAY D. SCRIBNER, and ALICIA PAREDES SCRIBNER, Eds.

Schools for Sale: Why Free Market Policies Won't Improve
America's Schools, and What Will
ERNEST R. HOUSE

Reclaiming Educational Administration as a Caring Profession
LYNN G. BECK

Cognitive Perspectives on Educational Leadership
PHILIP HALLINGER, KENNETH LEITHWOOD, and JOSEPH MURPHY, Eds.

SCHOOL CHOICE IN URBAN AMERICA

Magnet Schools and the Pursuit of Equity

Claire Smrekar
Ellen Goldring

TEACHERS
COLLEGE
PRESS

Teachers College, Columbia University
New York and London

Published by Teachers College Press, 1234 Amsterdam Avenue, New York, NY 10027

Library of Congress Cataloging-in-Publication Data

Smrekar, Claire.
    School choice in urban America : magnet schools and the pursuit of
equity / Claire Smrekar, Ellen Goldring.
        p.   cm. — (Critical issues in educational leadership series)
    Includes bibliographical references (p.   ) and index.
    ISBN 0-8077-3829-8 (cloth : alk. paper). — ISBN 0-8077-3828-X
(paper : alk. paper)
    1. Magnet schools—United States.   2. School choice—United
States.   3. School integration—United States.   I. Goldring, Ellen
B. (Ellen Borish), 1957–   . II. Title.   III. Series.
LB2818   1999
373.24'1'0973—dc21   98-52041

ISBN 0-8077-3828-X (paper)
ISBN 0-8077-3829-8 (cloth)

Printed on acid-free paper

Manufactured in the United States of America

06   05   04   03   02   01   00   99   8   7   6   5   4   3   2   1

Contents

Acknowledgments

This book evolved and was completed with the assistance, encouragement, and guidance of very generous people. We embarked on this study with the support of the Spencer Foundation. At Peabody College, numerous colleagues critiqued our work and kept us on track. Bill Hawley was central to the initial design and conceptualization of this project. Bob Crowson was always available to provide alternative perspectives and help us think carefully about our interpretations. Charles Hausman was a true partner and colleague, asking hard questions before looking at the data. Bob Saffold meticulously managed the data-collection efforts and ongoing communication with the districts. Jerome Morris, Lyda Philips, and Lora Vogel provided valuable research assistance.

Joe Murphy provided support as Chair of the Department of Educational Leadership, Teachers College Press Series Editor, and as a colleague.

Our colleagues William Taylor and Corrine Yu, from the Citizen's Commission on Civil Rights, kept us focused on the needs of poor children in urban districts and always asked the "so what" questions. We have learned to rely on and value their insights and their years of experience.

A book cannot be produced without enormous clerical support. Amanda McGill, LouAnn Bardash, and Danetta Mitchell all stayed with us as we drafted and redrafted.

Most importantly, we acknowledge the parents and teachers from Cincinnati and St. Louis. We thank the faculty and staff members of all the schools that participated in our study for their patience and cooperation. The experiences and perspectives they shared provided an enduring appreciation for the challenges of working in elementary schools. We also thank the parents who filled out surveys and shared their afternoons and evenings with us in lengthy discussions. We are grateful for the warmth and cooperation that accompanied these thoroughly enjoyable and valuable exchanges.

Introduction

Magnet schools are being introduced in more and more urban districts in an attempt to promote racial diversity and innovation, improve scholastic standards, and provide a range of curricular options to satisfy parents' interests and priorities. This book is designed to accomplish two goals: to examine in depth the policies and practices that shape magnet schools, and to contribute to the discourse among educational leaders, policymakers, and researchers regarding the meaning and importance of magnet schools to the experiences and opportunities of students and their families. The manuscript blends survey research with qualitative case studies to explore the serendipitous nature of school-choice, the teaching and learning context in magnet schools, and the paradoxical consequences of "unmaking community" for purposes of racial diversity and equity.

The interpretive text and explanatory focus of the book draw from the prevalent theories associated with school-choice debates to compare and contrast the predicted and actual consequences of school choices in urban districts. Rational choice (Elster, 1986), institutional (DiMaggio & Powell, 1991), and market theory (Friedman, 1955) provide frameworks for reviewing the numerous claims regarding the predicted dynamics of magnet school choice. This volume is not about the "choice" or "no choice" debate, but asks, given the nature and quality of magnet school plans in urban districts, can school-choice arrangements be designed to enhance equity and community in all our schools?

Over the last 3 years, with the support of the Spencer Foundation, we have investigated magnet and nonmagnet schools in two large urban school districts: St. Louis and Cincinnati. In each of these districts, we have conducted in-depth qualitative case studies and surveyed thousands of parents and teachers in elementary schools. The schools in these districts operate under carefully developed and regularly monitored choice plans and are part of stable, relatively well funded educational systems. In this sense, each school district reflects a "good case scenario" for realizing the potential claimed by advocates of school choice.

This volume provides a current and intensive analysis of the social and political context of magnet schools. Most research to date has relied on secondary analyses of data sets with important data unavailable, on case studies of particular schools that cannot speak to systemwide effects, or on official reports that deal mainly with design issues. Thus, despite the fact that half of all large urban school districts feature magnet programs, the empirical research on magnet schools remains relatively scant.

This book brings together empirical data and theoretical arguments that address the magnet school debate. Each chapter presents statistical analyses of the survey data from our two urban districts, comparing magnet school conditions and characteristics to nonmagnet schools. This comparison captures a broad overview of the magnet school context. Case-study and interview data are presented to provide in-depth portraits of children, families, and teachers, and to describe the life in magnet schools.

The first two chapters of the book investigate the case for magnet schools. Chapter 1, " School Choice in the Public Arena," outlines a set of key policy arguments and research findings in the area of school choice, with specific reference to magnet schools and their implications for families, communities, and schools (see Blank, Levine, & Steel, 1996; Metz, 1990). The critical gaps in understanding the nature and function of magnet schools are highlighted, with a particular emphasis on the political and social contexts of various districts that give rise to critical differences in admissions, transportation, and information systems across magnet school programs. The gaps in knowledge (what we know, what we *think* we know, what we *need* to know), measured against the backdrop of fervent public interest in school choice, frame the discussion for our extensive investigation into magnet school policies and practices. The chapter concludes with the specific questions to be addressed in subsequent chapters and a brief overview of our quantitative and qualitative research methodologies.

Chapter 2, "The Context of Magnet Schools: The Policies and Politics of Desegregation," examines the legal and historical context in which school-choice remedies were adopted in St. Louis and Cincinnati. This chapter is written by William Taylor and Corrine Yu, Vice Chair and Director, respectively, of the Citizen's Commission on Civil Rights, a bipartisan organization established in 1982 to monitor the civil rights policies of the federal government. Their analyses focus on the conditions of racial isolation and discriminatory practices that gave rise to federal court litigation in each of the school districts. This chapter establishes the prologue for a later discussion of the perverse consequences of school choice: the substitution of social-class segregation for racial segregation, when higher-status children attend magnet schools and lower-status children attend nonmagnet schools. The chapter concludes with a current overview of district demographics and system characteristics, including mechanisms designed to guard against resegregation.

In the next three chapters, which look at the promise and the reality of school choice, we begin to explore in depth the rich data from our study of two magnet school systems. Chapter 3, "Magnet Schools and the Social Context of School Choice," examines the decision-making context of parents in magnet school districts and the intersecting influence of social class, school characteristics, and school district dissemination activities on parents' decision making. How and why do families exercise their right to choose? What information do they use to make their choices? How is the decision-making context related to social class and ethnicity?

The findings from our research indicate that despite robust public information and dissemination efforts by school districts, serious issues related to social-class bias or "creaming" persist in these magnet school systems. This chapter demonstrates the important role of parents' primary social networks in the source, level, and type of information utilized in the context of choice. The context of decision making shifts from a singular, rational act to a process influenced by particularly salient properties of social-class position. This research underscores the ways in which social networks (associated with social class) provide access to the resources that are central for parents in managing the educational choices offered by some school districts.

Chapter 4, "Community or Anonymity? Patterns of Parent Involvement and Family-School Interactions in Magnet Schools," discusses the degree to which the norms and organizational arrangements in magnet schools contribute to family-community-school linkages. We examine issues of communication, parent-teacher value congruency, social cohesion, parental involvement, and commitment. Our findings indicate deep and enduring cleavages among magnet school parents that make occasions for face-to-face interaction typically brief, unpredictable, and unrelated. Varying degrees of integration and isolation among families of different social class and ethnicity emerge as fundamental public policy concerns that challenge the claims of magnet school proponents and critics alike. Against the backdrop of lower-than-expected levels of parent involvement in magnet schools and the potential loss of "shared spaces" in neighborhood "communities," this chapter provides a meaningful (and often missing) analysis of the key implications of building community in a district context of public school choice.

Chapter 5, "Magnet School Teachers and Their Workplace," highlights issues of classroom resources, curriculum, and teacher autonomy. Market theory suggests that a system of choice increases the innovation and diversity of curricular offerings and teaching methodologies. Similarly, it is argued that a market system creates an environment that encourages the growth of a number of diverse and innovative schools (e.g., see Chubb & Moe, 1990). In contrast, institutional theory (DiMaggio & Powell, 1991) predicts that the implementation of a system of choice based on magnet schools may constrain diversity and innovation because school boards and central office administration, rather than the clients (parents) and other stakeholders in education (Clinchy, 1989), continue to make decisions about curricular offerings.

This chapter describes the wide array of special themes and instructional philosophies offered in the magnet schools. However, the data from our research indicate that beyond the advertised themes, there are few substantive differences between magnet and nonmagnet schools in terms of the academic and extracurricular programs. Although magnet school teachers do seem to be flexible in terms of varying instructional strategies to meet students' learning styles, there are few differences between magnet and nonmagnet schools in the level of instructional resources such as librarians, art teachers, and other ancillary personnel. The findings also suggest that teachers in magnet schools work in a flexible, collaborative context.

We conclude the book with a look at new directions for magnet schools. Chapter 6, "Rethinking Our Choices," argues that the claims regarding the effects of parental choice on school improvement are both ambitious and controversial. As more and more districts across the United States introduce magnet schools, the need to assess the design and impact of these choice plans becomes paramount to the interests of parents, students, and policymakers.

This chapter summarizes the themes outlined in earlier chapters related to equity, community, and school organization. We call attention to the troubling indications of increasing resegregation along class lines, the loss of community and rootedness that once bound schools and neighborhoods in a sense of shared space and shared values, and the discouragingly thin and dry quality of parent involvement in schools of choice. The theoretical propositions linked to free-market arguments and institutionalization are assessed against the viewpoints expressed by the parents, teachers, and principals, whose experiences and expectations are at the center of our analyses. The chapter includes a cautionary note to educators and policymakers responsible for implementing magnet school plans: The way in which these plans are constructed must undergo extreme scrutiny.

The conclusion examines the public policy dilemmas embedded in the decisions to amplify the "democratic values" of individual choice in American schools. We underscore the irony of magnet school plans by juxtaposing the claims of school-choice advocates with the reality of exacerbated social-class differences in terms of access, opportunity, and understanding of school choice. We conclude by anchoring our critical analysis of the possible risks inherent in magnet school systems—through the elevation of choice and individual self-realization in public education—to the central themes in the recent research on the erosion of democratic institutions in America (e.g., Elshtain, 1995; Lasch, 1995).

School choice, community and parental involvement, and desegregation have headlined the national and state education reform agendas for the past decade. We hope readers find that this book offers a unique contribution to the policy discourse by integrating these often disconnected areas of research within one rigorous research study of two large urban school districts.

CHAPTER I

School Choice in the Public Arena

The claims made regarding the effects of parental choice on school improvement are both ambitious and controversial. Proponents of public school choice maintain that it promotes racial balance voluntarily rather than through court-ordered busing of children to distant schools in unfamiliar neighborhoods. They argue that it enhances academic excellence by making individual schools more focused on providing quality instruction in order to attract students. Finally, choice is seen as a way to counteract the effects of income level on educational opportunity, by establishing expanded options for lower-income families that are typically available only to wealthier families who are able to buy or rent homes in neighborhoods with more desirable schools.

Magnet schools, the focus of this book, are being established in more and more school systems in an attempt to improve scholastic standards, to promote diversity in race and income, and to provide a range of programs to satisfy individual talents and interests. Magnet schools, sometimes referred to as "alternative schools" or "schools of choice," are public schools that provide incentives to parents and students through specialized curricular themes or instructional methods. "Nonmagnet" schools as used in this text comprise the conventional zone schools in which children are placed by geographic conditions and not by choice. The term *magnet* gained popularity in the 1970s when policymakers were designing desegregation plans in an effort to make them more attractive to parents, educators, and students. Magnet schools provide school districts with an alternative to mandatory reassignment and forced busing by providing a choice for parents among several school options—each offering a different set of distinctive course offerings or instructional formats. In magnet schools, enrollments are regulated to ensure a racially balanced student population.

WHAT WE KNOW ABOUT MAGNET SCHOOLS

Since 1975, when federal courts accepted magnet schools as a method of desegregation (see *Morgan v. Kerrigan*), their number has increased dramatically. Indeed, between 1982 and 1991, the number of individual schools offering magnet programs nearly doubled to over 2,400 and the number of students enrolled in these programs almost tripled. By the 1991–92 school year, more than 1.2 million students were enrolled in magnet schools in 230 school districts (Yu & Taylor, 1997). As to the distribution of magnet schools, 85% are located in large (>10,000 enrollment) urban districts; 72% are located in high (>50%) minority districts; 55% are located in low (>50% Free Lunch Eligible) SES districts (Steel & Eaton, 1996).

Magnet schools are typically established in urban school districts with large student enrollments (over 10,000). According to the U.S. Department of Education, 53% of large urban school districts include magnet school programs as part of their desegregation plans, as compared with only 10% of suburban districts (Steel & Levine, 1994). Over half of all magnet programs are located in low socioeconomic districts (Levine, 1997). Although they can involve all grade levels, more than half of the nation's magnet programs serve elementary school students; only 20% of magnets are located at the high school level (Levine, 1997; Yu & Taylor, 1997). The most common type of magnet school is one that emphasizes a particular subject, such as math and science, computers and technology, or a foreign language. Following subject matter in terms of popularity are programs that offer a unique instructional approach, such as Montessori or Paideia.

Magnet school programs are extremely popular, as measured by the fact that over 75% of all districts with magnets have a greater demand for student slots than they can fill; half of these districts maintain long waiting lists (Blank, Levine, & Steel, 1996). With this level of demand, and with a total of over 15% of all students in magnet districts already enrolled in magnet schools, school districts must limit entry into the specialized programs. Most accomplish this through an admissions process that uses a lottery format. Others rely upon a first-come, first-served arrangement. Only about one-third of all magnet programs use a selective admissions policy; these usually involve a minimum test score requirement or, in a performing arts magnet, the admission may be based on performance in an audition.

In many instances, districts have supported magnet schools with a considerable investment of resources. On average, expenditures per student are 10% higher in districts with magnets; almost three-fourths of magnet programs have additional staffing allowances as well. Some magnet programs are funded through state desegregation funds. Most are funded under two-year grants through the federal Magnet Schools Assistance Program (MSAP). These funds are made available to districts that are either implementing magnets voluntarily or are acting under court-ordered desegregation. The MSAP serves a critical role in magnet school creation and expansion efforts nationwide. The program provides about $110 million annually to support magnet school programs; between 1985 and 1993, about $750 million in MSAP funds were allocated to 117 different school districts (Steel & Eaton, 1996).

WHAT WE *THINK* WE KNOW
ABOUT MAGNET SCHOOLS

As more and more urban school districts use magnet schools as a tool for desegregation and a mechanism for expanded public choice, the debates around issues of equity and excellence assume greater significance. How do magnet schools contribute to school improvement, enhanced community, and elevated trust in public education? Advocates of magnet schools argue that magnets: (1) attract students of different racial and socioeconomic backgrounds with similar educational interests; (2) provide unique sets of learning opportunities; and (3) encourage innovation. In other words, magnets are viewed as an effective way to enhance diversity and equity among schools, increase educational quality in a school district, and stabilize enrollments.

Research specifically addressing magnet schools, as compared with other school choice programs, is relatively limited. Mary Metz's *Different by Design* (1986) and Christine Rossell's *The Carrot or the Stick* (1990) are major empirical works focusing on magnet schools. Both of these books address questions of equity, access, and school choice and are widely cited in both academic and policymaking circles.

Other studies explore magnet schools in the context of national data sets. Using data from the National Educational Longitudinal Survey, Gamoran (1996) compared students in magnet schools with those in Catholic schools, nonreligious private schools, and public comprehensive schools. He reported some advantages for magnet school students in achievement in reading and history. Other researchers analyzed background characteristics of students in different school types, including magnet schools. They found that magnet schools enroll higher proportions of black and Hispanic students than do vocational-technical schools of choice (Plank, Schiller, Schneider, & Coleman, 1992). National data sets provide a broad overview of possible consequences of magnet schools. However, it is difficult to relate the findings to any particular local school district. Furthermore, it is difficult to explain how the results are related to specific magnet school policies.

In contrast to national data sets, there are evaluations of specific magnet school plans. Students in New York City's career magnet schools improved their reading achievement more than students who attended comprehensive schools (Crain, Heebner, & Si, 1992). In the Wake County public school choice system in North Carolina, the researchers surveyed parents, teachers, and students, focusing on satisfaction, access, and achievement (Valente, Jr., Applebaum, Larus, & Faldowski, 1989).

Many evaluation studies of magnet schools are not widely disseminated or published. To the best of our knowledge, there has not been a concerted effort to review collectively the large number of district-level evaluation documents. What we do know seems to come from political debate, educational forums, and the popular press. One of the most contested issues concerning magnet schools, for example, is the question of access and resources.

Critics of magnet school programs charge that magnets can exacerbate existing class or socioeconomic cleavages, especially when the magnets are academically selective and few in number. They assert that middle-class parents are more motivated and more informed regarding the availability of educational options, while lower-income parents opt for or otherwise "end up" in conventional attendance area schools with no specialized offerings and fewer resources. Thus, it is claimed that magnets tend to "cream off" more academically motivated and able students, as well as more effective and innovative teachers, resulting in diminished educational opportunities (e.g., less rigorous curricula, lower expectations by teachers, and different school climates) for those who do not attend them (Moore & Davenport, 1989). Further, critics of magnet schools argue that magnet schools divert resources that should be used for systemwide improvements and that there is little "spillover" from magnets because systems do not use them to foster the diffusion of innovation (Eaton & Crutcher, 1996).

WHAT WE *NEED* TO KNOW

As noted above, the empirical evidence on the effects of magnet schools remains relatively scant. Virtually all this research relies on secondary analyses of data sets with critically important data missing, on case studies of particular schools that cannot speak to school system-wide effects, on comparisons of public and private schools, or on official reports that deal with only some of the philosophical and design issues that are important to the development of policy and practice across school systems (see Metz, 1986; Steel & Eaton, 1996; Steel & Levine, 1994).

As the debate over the use of choice to improve schools intensifies and as the need to rely on magnet schools to achieve desegregation increases, three significant demographic trends complicate matters further. First, the nation's schools are becoming increasingly diverse—racially and ethnically; one-third of public school students are nonwhite (U.S. Bureau of the Census, 1996) (in this reference, "white" means non-Hispanic whites). Second, the proportion of the nation's children who live in poverty is growing; today, one in five children in the United States is poor (Zill & Nord, 1994). Third, the most recent report from the Harvard Project on School Desegregation indicates a steep backward slide toward segregation of African American and Latino students; these trends portend particularly pronounced segregation by social class (Orfield, Bachmeier, James, & Eitle, 1997). These developments indicate expanding racial and social isolation in America's public schools and city neighborhoods. They make it all the more important to estimate the consequences of parental choice on school enrollment patterns. These trends highlight the urgent need to ensure that increasing parental choice does not further disadvantage children who need high-quality education the most.

This book looks at the systemic use of magnet schools as examples of choice within public school districts. We are aware, of course, that the lessons of publicly regulated and managed parental choice plans cannot be generalized to choice plans that include private schools. Our analysis, however, sheds light on some of the assumptions underlying free-market approaches to choice because we have collected information on what kinds of parents choose magnet schools and the reasons they do so, as well as information on the characteristics of parents whose children are assigned, without choice, to neighborhood or zoned schools.

We have investigated the consequences of public school choice plans in communities where the plans have been carefully developed and monitored and where education is relatively well funded. We believe the litmus test of choice proposals is whether they serve the educational needs and interests of poor and minority children. Wealthier families have more latitude to buy or rent homes in the neighborhood or zone of a particularly desirable school. Accordingly, choice proposals should be evaluated in terms of their effects on those least able to exercise this kind of choice—those parents whose housing choices are severely constrained by income or persistent discrimination.

The focus of this study is on elementary magnet schools. We decided to study elementary schools for several reasons. The importance of schooling in the early years of development and its impact on later learning, future educational opportunities, and educational and occupational aspirations has been well documented (see Cross, 1994; Madden, 1993). In addition, much of the research on school choice and school community focuses on the secondary school level (see Bryk, Lee, & Holland, 1993; Coleman & Hoffer, 1987; Gamoran, 1996; Metz, 1986). Also, many districts that initially implemented magnet programs at the secondary school level have expanded their magnet programs to elementary schools. Today, more than half of all magnets are located in elementary schools. Only one-fifth are at the high school level (Blank, Levine, & Steel, 1996). Lastly, parents are typically more invested and involved in their children's education when students are young. Consequently, it may be most useful to attempt to understand the dynamics and consequences of magnet school choice at the elementary school level.

Our study examines various dynamics and outcomes of efforts to increase parental choice among public schools. The major questions addressed are:

1. *What is the context of decision making for parents in a system of school choice?* Who chooses magnet schools? What sources of information do parents use when making choices? Why do parents make the choices they do?

2. *What is the nature and quality of family-school interactions in magnet and nonmagnet schools?* Do relationships between parents and schools differ across social class, race, and ethnicity in magnet and nonmagnet schools, and is this interaction influenced by the social class, race, and ethnicity of parents and schools?

3. *Are there differences in the learning environments and workplace conditions between magnet and nonmagnet schools?* What is the nature of teaching and learning in magnet schools? What is behind the distinctive curriculum themes advertised in magnet programs?

Our study was conducted in the 1993–94 academic year in three cities with established magnet school programs: Cincinnati, St. Louis, and Nashville. This book presents the results from the Cincinnati and St. Louis segments of the study. We analyzed survey questionnaires from parents and teachers in both magnet and nonmagnet schools and conducted case studies in four magnet schools (see Research Methodology: Appendix A, for a complete discussion). Nashville's magnet system was undergoing fundamental changes during the year the study was conducted and for that reason its results are analyzed in a separate report.

OUR STUDY SITES

Cincinnati

During the 1993–94 school year, the Cincinnati Public School District operated 61 elementary schools, 8 junior high/middle schools, 10 secondary schools, and 7 special schools. Magnet (or what the Cincinnati system calls alternative) program choices were offered to students at all grade levels (K–12). The system operated a total of 51 alternative programs in 1993–94, including 26 separate program themes at 44 different school sites. (Note: Several sites operated with more than one program theme.)

In the Cincinnati system, magnet programs are differentiated by curriculum or special-interest areas as well as by instructional approach (for example, Montessori, Paideia). Magnets in the alternative program are also differentiated by enrollment structure and program coverage. The Cincinnati system uses four types of structures: (1) full, or dedicated, magnets enroll students strictly on the basis of a formal application and admissions process (described below) and provide alternative instruction to all students enrolled at the school site; (2) mixed magnets provide alternative instruction to all students enrolled at the school but enroll a combination of neighborhood/zoned students (because a percentage of the enrollment is reserved for zoned students) and students who have formally applied to the school but live outside the school's attendance zone (citywide application zone); (3) schools-within-schools are programmatically distinct components of a neighborhood school and provide alternative instruction only to those students who are enrolled in the magnet component based on their selection through the district's alternative school application process; (4) mixed schools-within-schools are a special version of schools-within-schools. They are organized within an existing neighborhood school and reserve a percentage of their enrollment capacity for zoned children, in addition to children living outside the attendance area.

Acceptance into magnet programs is based primarily on the application date (first-come, first-served) and race. Transportation is provided for students in grades K–8 who live more than one mile from their alternative school. Transportation is provided for all students in grades 9–12.

The system enrolled 46% of its students in magnet programs in the 1993–94 school year. Of those enrolled in magnets, 61.7% were African American. More than 43% of the district's African American students were enrolled in magnet programs in 1993–94. Total district enrollment in 1993–94 was approximately 51,000 (66% African American, 32% white, 2% other).

St. Louis

Under the provisions of a 1983 federal court order, the St. Louis City Public
School District operates an interdistrict voluntary transfer program that
includes magnet schools in the city. The interdistrict choice program allows
parents to choose between schools inside the district and some schools outside the district in order to promote racial balance. The consent decree,
which ended desegregation suits, involves heavy use of busing, with some
children spending as much as an hour on the bus morning and evening.

The St. Louis City District operates a total of 111 schools, including 73
elementary schools, 21 middle schools, 10 high schools, and 7 special schools.
The 16 suburban districts include approximately 109 elementary schools,
28 middle/junior high schools, and 26 high schools. The St. Louis City
District has 26 full-time and 2 part-time magnet programs within the city.
The district operates three different types of schools under the terms of its
desegregation plan: (1) magnet schools; (2) nonintegrated nonmagnet
schools that are 98% African American and located in predominantly African
American neighborhoods; and (3) integrated nonmagnet schools in or near
"naturally integrated" or transitional neighborhoods or achieved by busing.

Any student who lives in St. Louis and white students who live in the 16
participating suburban county districts may apply to the interdistrict transfer program. During the 1993–94 school year, 13,934 students were enrolled
in the transfer program between the city and the suburban school districts.
Of these, 12,775 African American city students transferred to suburban
county schools, while 1,159 county students transferred to the city to attend magnets. Transportation is provided for all city and county students
enrolled in the transfer program. County-to-city transfers were at an all-
time high in the 1993–94 school year, up 16% from the preceding year,
according to a March 1994 report from the Voluntary Interdistrict Coordinating Council (VICC, 1994). This agency oversees the settlement agreement that ended the desegregation suit.

The St. Louis City District has 26 full-time and 2 part-time magnet
programs ("schools of choice") within the city. Any student who lives in
St. Louis City and white students who live in the 16 participating suburban
county districts may apply. Assignments to magnets are made on the basis
of a general lottery, held in the spring. In 1993–94, the district enrolled
10,087 students in city magnets: 5,890 African Americans (58% of total
magnet enrollment) and 4,197 whites (42% of total magnet enrollment).
Total enrollment in St. Louis City Schools is approximately 36,091 of whom
78% are African American. Approximately 15% of the city's African American students are enrolled in city magnets, while 40% of the city's white

students attend city magnets. In the suburban districts included in the study, the school populations are about 25% African American.

Case Studies of Magnet Schools

- *Greenwood Paideia (Cincinnati).* Greenwood Paideia enrolls 378 students in grades kindergarten through six and is located near an industrial park in a racially mixed, middle-class section of the city about 20 minutes from downtown Cincinnati. Approximately 95% of the students are bused to Greenwood from neighborhoods across the city. The student population is 52% African American and 48% white. Forty-five percent of the students at Greenwood qualify for free lunch.
- *Mathematics and Science Academy of Cincinnati (MaSAC).* MaSAC enrolls 575 students in grades kindergarten through six, and is located in a working-class, predominantly white neighborhood on the western edge of the city. Approximately 83% of the students are bused to MaSAC from areas across the city. The school population is 51% African American and 49% white. Seventy percent of the students at MaSAC qualify for free lunch.
- *Overbrook Basic Academy (St. Louis).* Student enrollment at Overbrook rests at 253 and includes preschool through grade five. The student population is 60% African American and 40% white. Over 90% of the students who attend Overbrook are bused in from different neighborhoods across the city and county. Sixty-four percent of the students at Overbrook qualify for free lunch.
- *Viking Basic Academy (St. Louis).* Viking includes grades kindergarten through five and has a student enrollment of 298. The student population is 51% African American, 45% white, and 4% "other." More than 90% of the students are bused from various neighborhoods across the city and county. Sixty-eight percent of the students at Viking qualify for free lunch.

The next chapter expands the brief descriptive overviews of the school districts that are at the center of our examination of magnet schools by providing a deep and detailed legal history of school desegregation in Cincinnati and St. Louis.

CHAPTER 2

The Context of Magnet Schools:
The Policies and Politics of Desegregation
in Cincinnati and St. Louis

William L. Taylor and Corrine M. Yu

Long advocated by policymakers as a tool for voluntarily desegregating school districts, magnet schools have also been approved by the courts as a constitutionally permissible remedy to correct unlawful segregation in public school systems (see Rossell, 1990). Initially, when devices of massive resistance to desegregation began to fail in the early 1960s, some whites in the South turned to private choice in the form of segregation academies—often, although not always, established with religious backing. At the same time "freedom of choice" was widely adopted by school districts in the South as a device for limiting desegregation severely. Under these plans, parents would be required to choose among segregated and desegregated schools. White parents invariably chose white schools. Most African American parents in the South chose not to risk livelihoods or their lives by opting for desegregation. The Supreme Court put a stop to this in 1968 when it ruled in *Green v. New Kent County* that "freedom of choice" could be used only if it "promised to work" (i.e., desegregate the schools) and "work effectively now."

As desegregation moved north, however, and as the nation's affluence grew, choice became an important component in court orders and plans of the 1970s. Lacking public school options that appeared to offer educational advantages, many parents could choose private schools or relocate to suburbs that were often beyond the reach of desegregation orders. Unless attractive options were found within public schools systems, many feared that "white flight" would defeat desegregation plans. There evolved in desegregation planning the concept of "magnet schools," schools with educational offerings so promising that, it was hoped, parents would overcome their fears and concerns about interracial contact and place their children in

15

desegregated settings. In both St. Louis, Missouri, and Cincinnati, Ohio, magnet programs were established as a part of a desegregation remedy.

The St. Louis magnet program was first established in the mid-1970s, under a consent decree in a school desegregation lawsuit. Although the remedy in the decree was later broadened as the result of an intervention by the National Association for the Advancement of Colored People (NAACP), the magnet school program was continued by court order in 1980, and as a component of a 1983 settlement agreement, which also included a voluntary interdistrict transfer program with the St. Louis County school districts.

Magnet schools in Cincinnati, known as "alternative schools," were initially established after the filing of a desegregation lawsuit in 1974 and substantially expanded under a 1984 court order resulting from the settlement of the case.

In each case, the client community and the lawyers recognized early on the potential dilemma of solving one problem only to create another. An effort to minimize the danger of socioeconomic segregation was made by incorporating several provisions in the settlement agreements entered into by the parties. These included (1) the establishment of mechanisms for affirmative outreach in the form of recruitment and counseling centers designed to establish contact in all communities to inform parents and students of the new opportunities and to assure that students who selected the new schools would have counselors available if problems arose; (2) agreements that a significant number of magnets would be located in the inner city where they would be accessible to poor people; (3) agreements that transportation would be provided at no cost for all children; (4) agreements that with few exceptions (such as admission to a school for the performing arts or a program for the gifted and talented) the imposition of screening requirements for admission to magnets would not be allowed.

The St. Louis and Cincinnati lawsuits are among the longest running school desegregation cases in the federal courts. In this chapter we present the history of each of these cases and the context of the current magnet school plans. We discuss the racial isolation and discriminatory practices that gave rise to the federal court litigation in each of the school districts.

THE ST. LOUIS CASE

Missouri was one of the 17 Southern and border states that had school segregation laws in 1954. Prior to the Civil War, Missouri law (Act of 2/16/ 1847, §1) provided: "No person shall keep or teach any school for the instruction of Negroes or Mulattos, in reading or writing, in this state." Beginning in 1865, the Missouri General Assembly enacted a series of statutes requiring separate public schools for African Americans. This segregated system was incorporated into the Missouri Constitution of 1945, which specifically provided that separate schools were to be maintained for "white and colored children" (Article IX, Section 1A).

Statutes implementing the constitutionally mandated segregation provided for separate funding, separate enumerations, separate consolidated "colored" school districts, and interdistrict transfer of African American students. Most of these statutes were not repealed until 1957.

Under the state-mandated segregative system, white students were generally assigned to schools in their neighborhoods. Teachers and administrators were also segregated by law until 1954. State law additionally provided separate libraries, public parks, and playgrounds "for the use of white and colored persons,"and established separate "institutes for colored teachers."

In 1952, the Missouri Supreme Court upheld the constitutionality of Missouri law under the U. S. Constitution. Although a 1954 Attorney General Opinion declared Missouri law unenforceable following the first *Brown v. Board of Education* decision, the constitutional provision mandating separate schools for white and African American children remained a part of the Missouri constitution until 1976.

The St. Louis Board of Education's response to *Brown*—the adoption of a "neighborhood school" plan—did not change the segregated nature of the St. Louis school system. Under this plan, students were generally assigned to schools close to their homes. The school attendance zones that were drawn were nearly identical to the boundaries of racially identifiable neighborhoods. Moreover, students also had the option of electing a "continuation transfer" that permitted them to remain in the school in which they were then enrolled until graduation, unless overcrowding would result. This policy effectively preserved the pre-*Brown* system of student assignments and virtually guaranteed the plan's failure as a desegregation tool.

As was acknowledged in the desegregation litigation that later ensued, the effect of the city board's 1954–56 "neighborhood school plan" was to perpetuate the dual system by ensuring that most of the student population would continue to attend one-race or virtually one-race schools. Although the board kept no records of school racial composition from 1955 to 1962, 1962 records indicate that all 28 of the formerly African American elementary schools still in existence were all or virtually all African American; 36 other elementary schools were more than 90% African American. Similarly, 50 of the formerly white schools remained 85% or more white in 1962, and two-thirds of the white students attended schools that were 90% or more white.

In later years, the city board's segregative school assignment policy was enhanced by other board action that maintained and strengthened the dual school system. One such policy was a technique called "intact busing," which sent an entire class of students, everyday, with their teacher, from an overcrowded school to a vacant classroom elsewhere. Bused students were treated administratively as part of the school from which they came rather than the school to which they were sent, thus becoming an isolated subset of the school in which they were housed. While this technique was used in St. Louis pre-*Brown* to combat overcrowding by sending white children to white schools and African American children to African American schools, in the post-*Brown* era, most of the students affected were African American children bused to white schools.

Intact busing ceased in 1964 with the opening of 10 new schools. Segregation in student assignment continued, however. All of the 10 new schools that opened in 1964 were between 98.5% and 100% African American at the time of opening. Of the 36 elementary schools that were either newly constructed or newly opened between 1962 and 1975, 31 were more than 93% African American on opening and four were more than 94% white, with only one school that was integrated to any significant degree.

Despite the opening of these new schools, overcrowding still existed in some schools in the district. The city board's response to the overcrowding—"block busing"—also had a segregative effect. With block busing, students from certain blocks in the overcrowded school's attendance zone were sent to and incorporated into other schools. Although overcrowding existed in both African American and white schools, and both African American and white schools were available for transfer, very little white-to-African American busing occurred.

Another policy—"permissive transfer"—also helped perpetuate the dual school system. Under this policy, students could transfer out of their assigned schools to other schools in which space was available. Because the school district did not provide transportation until 1974, for many years the major beneficiaries of this policy were affluent white children (whose parents could provide transportation) who wanted to transfer out of their integrated school assignments to all-white schools.

In the 1970s, these practices were challenged successfully in an NAACP lawsuit and the courts ordered the implementation of an intradistrict remedy. By this time, however, the demography of the school district had changed drastically. More than 80% of the enrollment was African American and only limited desegregation was possible within the city's borders. (In fact, the court's approval of magnet schools in the city that were to have a 50–50 enrollment ensured that many other schools would be all African American.) Concerned about this, the Eighth Circuit Court of Appeals suggested the possibility of an interdistrict desegregation program in which the suburban districts in St. Louis County would participate voluntarily. Since the State of Missouri had been found to be a constitutional wrongdoer for its acts promoting segregated housing as well as schooling, the implication was that the state could be required to help pay for such a program if it did not participate voluntarily.

The suburban districts did not act on the court's suggestion, and in 1981, the city school board and the student plaintiffs filed a new complaint against the state and many suburban districts in St. Louis County seeking an interdistrict remedy. The board and the plaintiffs alleged that the state, the county districts, and others created and perpetuated interdistrict segregation and that consolidation of school districts was needed to remedy the effects of the constitutional violation.

On the eve of trial in 1983, all of the parties except the state reached the following settlement: (1) the suburban districts agreed to accept volunteering African American students until each had an enrollment of 25% African American students, which would then be maintained (since most of these districts had few African American students at the time, it was anticipated that about 15,000 seats would be made available under this arrangement); (2) the city board agreed to develop new magnet programs in the city and to accept volunteering suburban students into the program; and (3) the city board agreed to develop an extensive program of school improvements to serve students who did not participate in the transfer program or in magnet schools.

The district court and the Eighth Circuit Court of Appeals approved the settlement largely intact and implementation of the settlement agreement was ordered to commence with the 1983–84 school year. The Voluntary Interdistrict Coordinating Council (VICC) was established to assume the administrative responsibility for the implementation of the transfer components of the settlement agreement.

Over the next several years, the parties focused on the implementation of the settlement plan and on capital improvements. During this same time period, serious differences over the planning, funding, and operation of the magnet schools brought the parties—the state, city board, and county districts—into court again. To facilitate implementation of the magnet program, the Eighth Circuit Court of Appeals ordered the parties to prepare a plan to increase enrollment in the magnet program by 8,000 students by 1989–90. In 1988, after extensive review, evaluation, and recommendations by a group of court-appointed experts, the district court set forth a "long-term magnet school program . . . designed to eradicate, in part, vestiges of a segregated school system in the greater St. Louis area." This program required the city board to enroll, and the state and the board to fund, approximately 14,000 magnet students by the 1992–93 school year. The program also eliminated all distinctions between intradistrict and inter-district magnets.

Following the Court of Appeals' ruling, the city board worked to meet the court-imposed requirements that 14,000 students be enrolled in the magnet schools and 15,000 city students be enrolled in the county districts. In the midst of these efforts, and as capital improvements were ongoing, the state requested a hearing to determine whether the St. Louis public school system had achieved unitary status. In 1995, the district court granted the state's request for a unitary status hearing, and set a hearing date of March 4, 1996.

At trial, the state's expert witnesses claimed that desegregation had been carried out in good faith and that the remaining differences in aca-demic performance had to be due largely to differences in socioeconomic status between white and African American students, not to any wrong-doing by the schools. Plaintiffs' expert witnesses pointed to both local and national data suggesting that differences in socioeconomic status account for less than half of the difference in educational outcomes and suggested that school practices such as tracking must be considered in determining why the gap has not been narrowed further. The plaintiffs' experts also noted that African American transfer students were doing better in some suburban districts and schools than in others, suggesting further that school practices help determine educational outcomes.

When the trial concluded, the district judge suspended further pro-ceedings and appointed a settlement coordinator—Dr. William Danforth, former chancellor of Washington University in St. Louis—to seek a negoti-ated solution. The parties are now in the midst of formal negotiations.

Magnet Schools in St. Louis

During the 1993–94 school year, the city of St. Louis operated 28 magnet programs, spanning all grade levels. Magnets focus on different curricula and/or instructional approaches, including visual and performing arts, early childhood, math and science, and gifted education. The settlement pro-vides that a number of the magnet schools are to be located in the inner city so they are accessible to disadvantaged neighborhoods (Taylor, 1996). The magnet schools are open to any student in the city, as well as white students from the 16 suburbs that participate in the interdistrict transfer program. (Approximately 1,159 county students transferred to the city to attend magnet schools in 1993, about 25% of the white students enrolled in city magnets.) Assignments to magnets are made on the basis of a gen-eral lottery held in the spring. The racial balance of the magnet schools must be maintained so that none has an enrollment that is more than 60% or less than 50% African American (Board of Education, 1995). Overall, St. Louis enrolls approximately 11,000 students in city magnets, 18,000 in nonintegrated nonmagnet schools, and 11,500 students in integrated nonmagnet schools (Stevens, 1995).

The racial balance of the schools in St. Louis that participated in our study is consistent with the court decree. The racial balance of the 10 magnet schools in our study ranged from 61.8% to 51.1% African American students, whereas the integrated nonmagnet schools ranged from 88.4% to 25.5% African American students.

THE CINCINNATI CASE

Early in the 1960s, after the *Brown* (1954) decision but before the Supreme Court defined the constitutional obligations of northern school districts that did not have contemporary laws requiring school segregation, the NAACP brought a lawsuit in Cincinnati on behalf of African American schoolchildren, challenging the conditions of racial segregation that existed in the Cincinnati schools. The case was brought on a de facto theory, namely, that although evidence might be produced that public officials had deliberately segregated the schools, it was sufficient for the plaintiffs to show that a condition of segregation existed in the schools and that school authorities had failed to take corrective action. That theory was rejected in the federal courts in 1965 and the Cincinnati case (*Deal v. School Board*) was dismissed.

A new suit was filed by the NAACP on behalf of different plaintiffs in 1974, this time citing the segregation laws and policies that were pursued by the State of Ohio in the 19th century and contemporary practices by school officials, such as manipulating school zones, selecting sites for new schools, and assigning teachers to schools, that plaintiffs said evidenced a deliberate intent to racially segregate the schools. Much of the next 10 years was spent in technical legal proceedings addressing the issue of whether plaintiffs were precluded by the decision in the prior case from producing evidence to demonstrate that pre-1965 practices were racially motivated.

In 1984, on the eve of a trial that had long been delayed, a settlement of the case was reached by plaintiffs, the Cincinnati school system, and the State of Ohio. At the time, the Cincinnati system was a middle-sized urban district with a school population that was approximately two-thirds African American and one-third white. Although a substantial number of middle-class children attended the public schools, a large portion of the school system consisted of poor African American children and poor white children whose families had migrated from Appalachia. An effort to include the overwhelmingly white and middle-class suburban districts of Hamilton County in the case for the purposes of seeking more comprehensive relief had earlier been dismissed.

The Cincinnati settlement (*Bronson v. Board*) was built on two initiatives that had taken place after the case was filed. One was the initiation of a series of magnet schools and programs that the school system had begun in the early 1970s and intensified after the case was filed. This effort—dubbed "alternative schools" by the district—identified specialized themes or educational methodologies for particular schools and invited parents throughout the city to apply for them under guidelines designed to achieve racial balance.

Under the agreement, the alternative school program was greatly expanded to include 44 of the district's 85 school sites by the 1993–94 school year, serving approximately 40% of the school population. This made Cincinnati proportionately one of the largest magnet school programs in the nation. While desegregation could not have been accomplished without boundary changes, school closings, and a variety of other initiatives, the school board was able to trumpet the fact that a very large number of students were attending desegregated schools through the exercise of choice rather than through mandatory reassignments.

The second initiative was the adoption of the Taueber Index as the measuring rod of desegregation progress. The index measures the extent to which each school within a district reflects the racial composition of the district as a whole, and produces a single number between 0 and 100. An index of 100 reflects complete racial isolation, while an index of zero shows that each school mirrors the composition of the district as a whole. Civil rights and civic groups in Cincinnati adopted the index as a measure of whether the district was making progress in reducing the racial isolation of its schools. When the lawsuit was brought in 1974, the index was 76, reflecting a very high degree of segregation. By 1984, the index had been reduced to 53.

The settlement agreement established separate index targets for elementary, middle, and high schools in the mid-30s, within the range of what had been accomplished through court-ordered desegregation in other urban districts. The use of the Taueber Index afforded the Cincinnati School Board more flexibility than it might have had under a court order, which typically requires that most schools in a district reflect within specified percentage points (e.g., plus or minus 15) the racial composition of the district as a whole.

The settlement agreement was to last for 7 years, but has been extended twice. Among the continuing issues are a very high and racially disproportionate discipline rate. In 1991, despite provisions in the agreement calling for equitable administration of a discipline code, one child in five in the district was suspended or expelled, and the rate for African American children was twice that of whites.

While teacher union officials blamed the discipline problem on parents in low-income homes, some schools consisting entirely of disadvantaged children had high achievement rates and few suspensions or expulsions, while others suspended hundreds of students each year. This suggests that the key variable is not the student's socioeconomic status, but rather the ability of principals and teachers to establish an orderly environment for learning. The new settlement agreement enlists the services of the recently established Academy for Professional Development in assisting teachers in creating such an environment without suspending large numbers of students.

The new agreement also seeks to deal with the failure of a school system to raise achievement at several racially isolated schools serving low-income families that had been targeted by the earlier settlement for special efforts. Only one of eight such schools showed significant improvement in the performance of students over the life of the agreement. The new settlement includes an agreement on the part of the school district to require school personnel to be accountable for results.

After the Taueber Index goals were reached (36.5 for elementary schools, 36 for middle schools, and 34 for high schools), the school district was released from strict requirements that the goals be maintained. Instead, the superintendent and the board agreed to follow a process to seek to avoid resegregation. By 1995, however, the elementary and high schools had slipped to Taueber levels in the 40s, partially as a result of the board's decision to create duplicative magnets and to allow attendance on a neighborhood basis. Few steps had been taken to prevent resegregation from occurring. Plaintiffs in the case are now seeking a review by the State Superintendent of Public Instruction, pursuant to the current settlement agreement, of the city board's compliance.

Magnet Schools in Cincinnati

In the Cincinnati system, magnet programs are differentiated by curriculum or special-interest areas, as well as by instructional approach (Montessori, Paideia). Magnets in the alternative program are also differentiated by enrollment structure. The Cincinnati system uses four types of structures: (1) Full or dedicated magnets enroll students strictly on the basis of a formal application and choice process; (2) mixed magnets enroll a combination of neighborhood/zoned students and those who choose the school but live outside the school's attendance zone; (3) schools-within-schools are programmatically distinct components of a neighborhood school and provide magnet themed instruction to only those students who choose the magnet program; (4) mixed schools-within-schools are special versions of schools-within-schools. They are organized within existing zone schools and reserve a percentage of their enrollment for zoned children and choice children.

Acceptance to all programs is based on the application date (first come, first-served) and race. Overall, the system enrolled 46% of its students in magnet programs in the 1993–94 school year. Of those enrolled in magnets, 61.7% were African American. More than 43% of the district's African American students were enrolled in magnet programs, while 66% of the total district enrollment is African American. The racial balance of the magnet schools that participated in our study ranges from 56.9% to 46.2% African American, while the nonmagnet schools range from a high of 85% African American to a low of 30.4% African American.

CONCLUSION

For two decades, schools districts around the country, including St. Louis and Cincinnati, have established and conducted magnet schools as a means of achieving desegregation. With heavy involvement from the courts, these magnet schools are designed to meet constitutional and policy requirements to end racial isolation. In both Cincinnati and St. Louis, magnets have helped to achieve a high degree of racial desegregation. In Cincinnati, the percentage of African American students enrolled in the magnet programs is roughly the same (62%) as the total percentage of African American students in the district. In St. Louis, desegregation was more difficult to achieve. At the beginning of the litigation in the middle 1970s, the city schools were more than 80% African American. Today, with the combination of magnet schools, interdistrict transfers, and integrated nonmagnet schools, nearly 60% of all African American students attend desegregated schools (see Table 2.1).

The desegregation statistics in St. Louis and Cincinnati lend support to conclusions reached by Rossell (1990) in her comprehensive examination of voluntary desegregation plans: "Racism is not so deeply embedded in American society that substantial proportions of Americans cannot be persuaded to enroll their children voluntarily in desegregated

Table 2.1 The Enrollment of African American Students in Different Types of St. Louis Public Schools

	Percentage	Number of Students
Magnet Schools	15.0	6,646
Interdistrict Transfer Program	28.5	12,593
Integrated Neighborhood Schools	15.9	7,009
Non-Integrated Neighborhood Schools	40.6	17,915
TOTAL:	100.0	44,163

Source: Report from the Civic Progress Task Force on Desegregation of the St. Louis Public School System, Park I, December [Department of Justice Exhibit No. 90, *Liddell v. Board of Education,* E.D.Mo. No. 72-100 (c)(6), filed March 1996]["Civic Progress Report"].

magnet schools" (p. 216). What are the consequences and implications of these types of magnet plans? Are they equitable? Do they contribute to strong family-school-community linkages? Do they foster curricular innovation and unique teacher work contexts? In the next three chapters of this volume, we turn to the empirical exploration of our data to address these questions.

CHAPTER 3

Magnet Schools and the
Social Context of School Choice

The central debate regarding the conduct and character of magnet schools is framed by concerns related to equity and fairness. These debates are well known and well understood. Controlled-choice arrangements such as magnet schools may be assessed in terms of the degree to which they address the educational needs and interests of *all* students. A central mechanism in this "test of equity" involves providing information that is both accessible to and understandable by all parents, and that allows parents (not just the most sophisticated or well-educated) to make informed decisions about where their children will go to school. The standard and acceptable measure of equity, then, seeks to serve and benefit all students, regardless of racial, ethnic, or socioeconomic status (Glenn, McLaughlin, & Salganik, 1993; Moore & Davenport, 1989). Information of this character advises parents regarding the supply of educational options, such as the content of specific programs, and is crucial to the demand side of magnet school choice and the way in which parents exercise and express their choices (Salganik & Carver, 1992).

Critics of school-choice plans often point to the issue of access to information as one of the major sources of inequity under magnet school programs. These analysts suggest that economically disadvantaged families do not have adequate access to information, may not be aware of their options for choice, and may not have the formal and informal networks to learn about alternatives (Moore & Davenport, 1989).

Rational choice theory suggests that individual families that exercise their right to make choices rationally weigh the various alternatives in conjunction with their own values and preferences. Rational choice theory implies that parents reflect on their values and the needs of their children and articulate their preferences through the choices they make. They look for schools that offer programs that are congruent with their values and the perceived learning needs of their children, weighing costs and benefits

(Archbald, 1988; Coons & Sugarman, 1978). Rational choice theory assumes that the consideration of alternatives occurs with accurate and adequate information.

The major questions addressed in this chapter are: Who chooses magnet schools? How are choices made? For what reasons? What sources of information do parents use when choosing schools? How does social-class position influence the source, nature, and quality of information parents utilize in this context? How do neighborhood stability and isolation, limited access to transportation and civic organizations, and occupations that disallow workplace associations impact low-income parents' primary social networks? Are district- and magnet school–level information-dissemination activities, such as mailings, meetings, and media outreach, effective in providing information on choice options to all parents? The analysis and discussion provide a framework to examine rational choice theory. Our results suggest that the context of parental decision making is more complex than a singular, individual rational act. Parental choice is part of a social process influenced by salient properties of social-class position.

WHO CHOOSES MAGNET SCHOOLS?

Cincinnati's magnet school parents, across both white and African American groups, have higher income levels than do parents in nonmagnet schools. According to our surveys, over one-third of the magnet school parents have annual incomes above $50,000, compared with just 18% of the nonmagnet school parents. Conversely, one-fourth of the magnet school parents have general household incomes below $15,000, compared with 44% of the nonmagnet school parents. Among African American parents in the Cincinnati magnet schools, 34% have income levels below $15,000, compared with 54% in nonmagnet schools, and 29% have incomes above $50,000, compared with 11% in nonmagnet schools. Similar trends are evident for white parents: 17% of white parents in magnet schools have household incomes below $15,000, compared with 33% in nonmagnet schools and 36% have incomes above $50,000, compared with 23% in nonmagnet schools. Information obtained from principals about their schools indicates that, on average, 49% of the students enrolled in magnet schools receive free or reduced-price lunch, compared with 80% of the students in nonmagnet schools (see Table 3.1).

Similar trends are evident in regard to the educational level of parents. Parents in Cincinnati's magnet schools, across all racial groups, are more likely to have higher educational levels than their counterparts in nonmagnet schools. For example, 21% of the magnet school parents in our survey are college graduates, compared with 12% of nonmagnet school parents; only 11% of the magnet school parents have not completed high school, compared with 27% of nonmagnet school parents. This trend is similar for both African American parents and white parents. Among African American parents in magnet schools, 20% are college graduates and 14% hold graduate degrees; in nonmagnet schools, 15% are college graduates and only 1% hold graduate degrees. Among white parents in magnet schools, 23% are college graduates, compared with 9% in nonmagnets.

Parents in Cincinnati magnet schools are more likely to be employed than are parents in nonmagnet schools. In magnet schools, 13% of the parents indicate that neither parent is employed (either full- or part-time); this unemployment rate is double (26%) for nonmagnet school parents. Among African American parents in magnet schools, 17% indicate that neither parent is employed, compared with 29% in nonmagnet schools. Among white parents in magnet schools, 9% are unemployed, compared with 23% of the white parents in nonmagnet schools.

In general, similar patterns of enrollment are found in St. Louis (see Table 3.1). One-third of magnet school parents in St. Louis earn less than $15,000 annually. This is in stark contrast with nonmagnet school parents— 68% of whom earn below $15,000. Nonmagnet school parents are also more likely to be unemployed. Similarly, St. Louis magnet school parents are al-

Table 3.1 Summary of Socioeconomic Status of Parents in Cincinnati and St. Louis (percentage of respondents)

	Cincinnati		St. Louis		
				Nonmagnet	
	Magnet	Nonmagnet	Magnet	Integrated	Nonintegrated
Income Levels					
Below $15,000	24.9	43.7	32.2	67.5	62.7
Educational Levels					
College Degree	21.2	11.9	22.4	7.5	11.3
Graduate Degree	18.0	7.0	11.0	2.7	4.0
Free Lunch					
Qualified for Free Lunch	49.0	80.0	71.0	95.0	97.0
Family Structure					
Married	63.0	44.5	55.0	26.5	21.3
Single, Never Married	9.7	20.4	13.0	33.2	43.6
Both Parents					
Unemployed	12.6	25.7	11.3	38.2	39.8

Data: Self-Reports from Parent Surveys; *see* Appendix A

most three times as likely to hold college degrees when compared with nonmagnet parents in St. Louis.

In summary, although the racial composition of many magnet and nonmagnet schools is similar, it is clear that magnet schools enroll students whose parents are of higher socioeconomic status with regard to income, education, and employment. These differences are consistent for all racial groups.

Our data support the concerns of many that school choice can lead to public schools segregated according to social class, and become the mechanism for a "new improved sorting machine" (Moore & Davenport, 1989). These findings are consistent with data from other districts across the United States. For example, in a review of five choice programs—Minnesota's Open Enrollment Option, San Antonio's Independent School District's Multilingual Program, Milwaukee's Voucher Plan, and two privately funded choice programs—Martinez, Thomas, and Kemerer (1994) conclude that parents who choose schools are "better educated, have higher incomes, and are less likely to be underemployed than nonchoosing parents" (p. 679). In more recent studies, similar patterns have been found. For example, in Minnesota, Tenbusch (1993) found that parents with more education were more aware of open enrollment options. Similarly, Archbald's (1996) study of the Milwaukee magnet school program found that "clearly, in this district, there is evidence that, other things equal, neighborhoods with higher proportions of college educated adults enroll more students in magnet schools" (p. 158). Our findings are also consistent with the conclusions of the Carnegie Foundation for the Advancement of Teaching report (1992) suggesting that school choice seems to be an option for better-educated and higher-income families.

Although alarming, these findings are interpreted with less concern by some researchers. For example, supporters of school-choice plans claim that the long-term consequences of "white flight" and the loss of affluent parents to private and suburban schools offset the consequences of social-class segregation (Archibald, 1996; Rossell, 1990). It is also suggested that we should not perpetuate the myth that neighborhood assignment and busing result in equitable schools and, thus, school choice does not promote any more or any less inequality than mandatory assignment. As Clark (1989) notes: "Behind the bureaucratic pretense that comprehensive schools are equal schools lies the unquestionable fact that millions of students from poor and minority families living in poor neighborhoods are held captive in schools that are nowhere near as good as those found in well-off neighborhoods" (p. 110).

Explanations for this "creaming effect" include such issues as access to information, availability of transportation, and location of schools. It has been suggested that one avenue to help reduce social-class differences in a system of school choice is the availability of a complete system of information dissemination to encourage *all* parents to exercise choice. Our findings indicating differences in the socioeconomic status of magnet parents and nonmagnet parents underscore the importance of applying a "test of equity." These issues are addressed more fully in a later section in this chapter.

WHY PARENTS CHOOSE

Why do parents choose alternatives to their neighborhood schools? Empirical studies of various choice plans, including research on magnet schools, suggest a complex array of reasons (see Goldring & Hausman, 1996). The complexity seems to converge around a number of central questions: Do parents choose for academic reasons or convenience reasons? Is convenience a proxy for safety and for parents' familiarity with the neighborhood? Furthermore, do parents choose alternatives to allow their children to learn with others from "similar" or "higher" social-class backgrounds?

The Carnegie Foundation survey (1992) found that few parents—only 15%—cited academic issues as their main reason for considering an alternative school for their child. Similarly, a study of Minnesota's open-enrollment plan reported that only 20% of participating parents chose for academic reasons, while 40% of the parents mentioned convenience as their main reason for choosing an alternative school for their child (Minnesota House of Representatives, 1990). In contrast, Fossey (1994) found that parents participating in the Massachusetts interdistrict choice plan did not choose for convenience, but made "rational decisions when transferring their children out of their home communities, choosing districts with higher indicators of student performance and higher socioeconomic status than the districts they left" (p. 331). This view is supported by a recent study by Wells and Crain (1997) of African American parents from St. Louis who chose to send their children to suburban county schools. These parents perceived that the county schools were better than the city schools. "Whether these parents and guardians are completely accurate in their assessment of the quality of the country schools, the fact that they cited resources and achievement-oriented factors, as opposed to the proximity and familiarity factors cited by the parents of students in the city schools, makes an important statement" (p. 206).

Parents may make school choices based on the social and racial makeup of the student body. In case studies of three magnet schools, Metz (1986) reported that one magnet school "developed a long waiting list because many middle-class and ambitious working-class parents sought a school where their children would be with the children of the highest social class and achievement level possible" (p. 208). In contrast, Rossell (1990) suggests that to understand parents' choice-making as it pertains to race and social class, it is important to explore the curriculum of the magnet schools as well as the racial makeup of the neighborhoods where the magnet schools are situated, and the racial composition of the schools themselves. In a review of 20 magnet programs, Rossell found that "whites will transfer to minority schools only if the districts put additional funds and a special curriculum there" (p. 145).

Another perspective suggests that parents do not choose schools so much as they leave other schools behind. This view argues that parents participate in school-choice plans because they have a general sense of dissatisfaction with their previous school. Witte, Bailey, and Thorn (1993) found that parents who participated in the Milwaukee voucher experiment were very dissatisfied with their local public schools. In a review of choice plans, Martinez, Thomas, and Kemerer (1994) reported that parents who choose alternative schools are more dissatisfied with their previous school than are parents who opted not to participate in the choice plans.

This research is consistent with our findings from both the surveys and the case studies. When we asked parents in our study to identify the issues that were important to them in selecting a magnet school for their child, most reported the academic reputation of the school, teaching style, and transportation (see Table 3.2). A review of the conceptual and empirical literature indicates four broad categories of parents' reasons for school choice (Bauch & Small, 1986). These dimensions include academic and curricular, discipline and safety, religion and social values, and transportation/proximity/convenience. We explicated and expanded these four dimensions to include 21 items based on a review of other survey instruments and a pilot test of our own questionnaires.

Satisfaction

Our data also clearly indicate that parents who are most dissatisfied with the schools in their communities are most likely to choose magnet schools. For example, in St. Louis, 59% of magnet school parents gave the schools in their community a grade of C, D, or F. Furthermore, the data suggest that the higher the income of the parents, the higher the level of dissatisfaction with public schools in the community. Moreover, whites expressed more dissatisfaction with the community's schools than did African Americans. Again in St. Louis, African Americans accounted for 75% of the magnet school parents who rated the schools in the community with an A, while

Table 3.2 Parents' Reasons for Choosing a Magnet School (percentage of respondents)

Reason for Choice:	Cincinnati	St. Louis
Academic Reputation	72.0	62.0
Teaching Style	64.7	53.9
Transportation	50.7	42.6
Teachers	40.9	33.1
Near Home	32.5	18.6
Racial/Ethnic Mix	44.4	36.3
School Shares Values	42.7	31.7
Parent Involvement	39.5	23.2
Discipline	37.8	30.9
Safety	31.1	28.6
Another Child at School	35.0	18.8
Principal	32.9	23.0
Individual Help	29.0	39.8
Special Programs	32.2	48.9
Like the Neighborhood	19.2	19.4
Near Child Care	0.7	1.0
Child's Friends	14.0	9.8
Smaller Class Size	14.7	28.0
Special Needs Services	8.0	21.7
Near Job	8.0	4.6
Before/After Care	1.4	0.4

Data: Self-Reports from Parent Surveys; *see* Appendix A

whites in magnet schools accounted for 59% of the parents who gave the schools a grade of D or F. These findings are supported in a study by Lee, Croninger, and Smith (1994) in their research on Detroit's interdistrict choice plan, where they found that "opinions about choice are driven by negative views of the quality of local schools" (p. 433).

Transportation

Without question, transportation is a major issue for many parents when choosing a school (Clewell & Joy, 1990). Although public transportation is provided by the school systems in both Cincinnati and St. Louis, many parents are uneasy about using this means of transportation, due to safety concerns and the length of time required to ride on the bus each day. We asked parents if there were public schools in the district that they did not consider due to transportation. Fourteen percent of the parents in Cincinnati and 42% of the parents in St. Louis answered yes to this question. Minority parents in both St. Louis and Cincinnati are significantly more likely than white parents to indicate that transportation is an issue. White parents in magnet schools are the least likely to indicate that transportation is a consideration in choosing a school (because, as indicated below, they are more likely to choose a school closer to their home). Additionally, and perhaps predictably, lower-income parents are more likely than upper-income parents to be concerned about transportation.

Academic Reputation

Social-class position seems to influence parents' reasons for choosing a magnet school. For instance, higher-income parents in both St. Louis and Cincinnati are significantly more likely to choose schools because of the academic reputation of the school. For example, 74% of St. Louis parents with incomes over $50,000 indicated that they chose a magnet school because of academic reputation, compared with 26% of lower-income parents. This finding supports research by Rossell (1990) that higher-income parents will choose urban magnet schools if they perceive there is a "good" academic program for their children.

In magnet schools, race influences some reasons for choice. Both white and African American parents are equally likely to choose magnet schools because of academic reputation. However, white parents in Cincinnati magnet schools, for example, are significantly more likely to choose a magnet school because it is located near their home (50.7% white compared with 15% African American). This finding is also supported by the Rossell (1990) study. She reported that the longer the bus ride, the lower the percentage of the opposite race enrolled in the magnet school. Accounting for racial segregation of housing, whites in Cincinnati are more likely to attend magnet schools closer to their homes rather than to choose a magnet school that would require a longer bus ride.

Together, these results paint a complex picture of why parents choose magnet schools. Parents seek good academic programs for their children, and are looking for alternatives due to a certain level of dissatisfaction with the other public schools. Simultaneously, parents are keenly aware of the practical issues that confront them when choosing a school further away from their homes. Parents who are upper middle class, who own their own cars, and who have flexibility in their schedules can more readily avail themselves of a wide array of choices without concern or dependence on the public system of busing. It would be a misinterpretation of our data to suggest that parents choose schools for academic reasons or proximity or convenience reasons. Rather, our data suggest that parents choose for academic *and* convenience reasons.

HOW DO PARENTS CHOOSE?

Much of the theoretical underpinning for parental choice in education is rooted in rational choice theory. Although rational choice theory is often termed "economic" in its approach to human behavior (Becker, 1986), the theory emerged from concepts in political science and is focused on individual decision making in a nonmarket system (Almond, 1990).

The core concepts in rational choice theory are individualism and interest maximization. Individuals are viewed as rational decision makers who act out of self-interest; they choose alternatives that provide the highest benefit based on individual preferences (Ostrom & Ostrom, 1971). Accordingly, in the context of school choice, parents will rationally weigh various educational options and alternatives and make choices that maximize their own goals. Rational choice theory implies that "parents will reflect upon their values and the needs of their children and will articulate their preconceived preferences regarding education . . . and, in doing so, will weigh costs and benefits" (Goldring & Shapira, 1993, pp. 397–398).

The concept of individualism is central to rational choice theory. Tversky and Kahneman (1986) suggest that individuals utilize varying "decision frames" or perspectives when they confront a choice. "The frame that a decision maker adopts is controlled by the norms, habits and personal characteristics of the decision maker" (p. 121).

Much of the recent critique of rational choice theory focuses on the failure to take account of the social, political, and organizational contexts in which decisions are made. As Cibulka (1996) notes, "If preferences are determined in a social context, utility maximization must be portrayed as a dynamic and fluid process" (p. 9). Other theorists have underscored the importance of expanding rational choice theory to consider complex decision-making contexts that include more than the individual decision maker. March (1986), for example, extends the notion of individual rationality to include those aspects that are highly embedded in specific social contexts. This context in which individual decisions are made is influenced by a network of social relationships with others. Coleman (1990) argues that when individuals are faced with important decisions, "a rational actor will engage in a search for information before deciding" (p. 238). As the rational actor seeks information, he or she will confer with others and begin to place trust in their judgments. Therefore, when many people are making similar decisions at a similar time, these individuals begin to depend on one another for information and judgment. Coleman suggests that these types of exchanges, geared toward satisfying individual interests, lead to the formation of social relationships or social networks. The exchange of information and judgments serves as a crucial basis for making decisions, but also provides a social context for making these decisions. Coleman concludes, "There is a broadly perpetrated fiction in modern society. . . . This fiction is that society consists of a set of independent individuals, each of whom acts to achieve goals that are independently arrived at" (p. 300). Coleman's analysis of individuals' sharing information and judgments to make decisions in a context of social networks suggests that individuals do not act independently.

Sources of Information

The survey and interview data we collected from parents regarding sources of information utilized in Cincinnati and St. Louis magnet schools indicate information access and collection patterns ranging from predictable and stable sources to a more serendipitous or unguided search. Table 3.3 indicates that in total, across all social classes, parents use social networks as a

Table 3.3 Information Used by Magnet Parents when Choosing a School (percentage of respondents)

Source of Information	Cincinnati	St. Louis
Talks with Teachers	38.7	42.0
Talks with Friends	56.7	43.4
Their Fifth Grade Child	35.8	49.7
Other Child's Experience	29.9	20.0
Other Family Members	19.5	16.6
School Newsletter	9.0	31.5
Informational Meetings	16.3	13.5
Radio, TV, Newspaper	3.5	10.7
Visit to Schools	44.5	38.0
Informational Center	9.9	23.3
Achievement Test Scores	29.4	16.8

Data: Self-Reports from Parent Surveys; *see* Appendix A

source of information about school choice more often than they use information formally disseminated. For example, 57% of all parents in Cincinnati indicated that they talked with friends, while only 10% utilized informational centers or schools. Similarly, parents in St. Louis rely on friends when choosing a school. Some parents in St. Louis also utilize official district information, such as newsletters and information centers.

Our survey research suggests that higher-income families utilize a wider array of resources more frequently than lower-income families (see Tables 3.4 and 3.5). These findings are consistent with data from controlled-choice programs in Milwaukee (Archbald, 1988) and in Montclair, New Jersey (Carnegie Foundation for the Advancement of Teaching, 1992), that indicate that income and education are influential elements in the context of parents' information-collection process. Higher-income families are more likely than lower-income families to use discussions with friends and teachers as sources of information; these parents are also more likely to use school visits and achievement tests scores when they are choosing a school for their children. Although lower-income families also utilize friendship networks in the process of school choice, they do so less frequently and at lower rates.

Table 3.4 Sources of Information Used by Magnet Parents by Income—Cincinnati

	Income			
Source of Information	Low <14,999	Medium <24,999	Medium High <49,999	High +50,000
Talks with Teachers*	32.1	28.3	43.8	45.0
Talks with Friends*	46.4	51.7	66.3	60.0
Your Fifth Grader	31.0	35.0	36.3	39.2
Other Child's Experience	22.6	23.3	31.3	37.5
Other Family Members	19.0	16.7	26.3	16.7
School Newsletter	13.1	8.3	6.3	8.3
Informational Meetings	15.5	6.7	16.3	21.7
Radio, TV, Newspapers	4.8	0.0	3.8	4.2
Visit To Schools*	27.4	26.7	51.3	60.8
Informational Center	8.3	5.0	13.8	10.8
Achievement Test Scores*	19.0	18.3	31.3	40.8

*$p < .05$
(Percentages are parents from the income group using a particular source of information.)

Table 3.5 Sources of Information Used by Magnet Parents by Income—St. Louis

	Income			
Source of Information	Low <14,999	Medium <24,999	Medium High <49,999	High +50,000
Talks with Teachers*	35.3	33.0	51.1	53.8
Talks with Friends	38.1	36.9	51.9	48.1
Your Fifth Grader*	42.4	40.8	58.5	63.5
Other Child's Experience	18.0	19.4	20.7	25.0
Other Family Members	18.7	16.5	14.1	17.3
School Newsletter	33.1	33.0	31.9	23.1
Informational Meetings	10.1	11.7	17.0	17.3
Radio, TV, Newspapers	7.2	8.7	14.8	13.5
Visit To Schools*	31.7	31.1	42.2	57.7
Informational Center	19.4	24.3	23.7	30.8
Achievement Test Scores*	15.1	9.7	20.7	25.0

*$p < .05$

(Percentages are parents from the income group using a particular source of information.)

Neighborhoods, Networks, and Knowledge

Consistent with our survey results and Coleman's (1990) conceptualization of rational choice theory, the findings from the qualitative multiple-case studies indicate that parents' social networks play a central and fundamental role in the source and type of information utilized in the context of choice. These networks indicate the importance of information gathering and exchange when parents participate in choice decisions. These pervasive patterns of information exchange further shatter the myth of independent, isolated action in the context of decision making.

During extensive interviews with magnet school parents, there were repeated references to co-workers, kin, and in some cases "the woman down the street" as sources of information regarding the magnet program and specific magnet schools. The "word-of-mouth" channel was underscored and distinguished from more deliberate district- and magnet school–level information-dissemination activities, such as mailings, meetings, and media outreach. As one magnet school parent noted, "I know it gets into the paper, but unless that is something you are looking for, you don't see it." Although most parents reported that they are aware of district- and school-level policies designed to provide accurate and accessible information to parents regarding magnet school choices, these sources are far less salient than parents' social and professional networks.

As this and other studies indicate, the nature and function of parents' primary social networks is directly related to social class (see Lareau, 1989; Useem, 1991). That is, the development and utilization of parents' social networks are linked to issues of occupation/employment status, neighborhood stability and isolation, and membership in recreation and community organizations (Cochran, 1990; Cochran & Brassard, 1979; Stanton-Salazar & Dornbusch, 1995). For example, several parents noted that information regarding the magnet system was more easily collected due to their own or a relative's employment status in the school district. Jacqui Adams, a Head Start director with a daughter enrolled in the math and science magnet school in Cincinnati (MaSAC), noted:

> The only reason that I know as much as I do is not just because I'm a concerned parent. There are a lot of concerned parents out there. The only reason that I know is because I'm part of the [school] system.

Jacqui's network includes principals, counselors, and school board members. She described the benefit of this kind of "insider information":

> I can ask the kinds of questions to get the information that I need to help me make informed decisions. That is the same thing I try to urge other people. If you don't know what you want, then you need to talk to people so that you are given the best information you can get and make the best decision that you can with what information you have.

Another parent whose three children attend magnet schools in Cincinnati reported that he routinely "checks things out" with a co-worker at his satellite television company; this co-worker also happens to be a school board member. Verda Jackson, a senior executive at the Urban League, noted that she talked to several people before enrolling her son at MaSAC four years ago. She recalled a specific conversation she had with a colleague at the Urban League:

> This person happened to be another parent, but also at the time she happened to be the education director here. She has had a lot of working relationships with different principals over the years, and is well known at the Board of Education because she has worked on a number of programs. I asked her about the particular

MaSAC program. She knew both the principal at the school and the program.

Many of the magnet school parents in St. Louis utilized similar information resources related to workplace and kin networks. Although these parents are aware of the district's pamphlets on magnet schools and have read newspaper articles about magnets, they sought the advice of kin and employees when, as one parent put it, "we were stumped." Terrell Jefferson, an electronics engineer and a father of two children at Overbrook Basic Academy in St. Louis, explained:

> When we first started, we talked to different people. There are a lot of people that we know who are in the school system here. We know someone who works for the board of education, so we always deal with him.

In selecting the magnet school over their neighborhood school, the Jeffersons also consulted with Terrell's two cousins, both of whom are teachers in a local school district.

Several parents noted the easy and convenient contact they enjoy with other parents in the neighborhood, whom they have known for a number of years; many of the children in the neighborhood are regular visitors to their homes. The neighborhood associations, local playgrounds and swimming pools, and community soccer teams provide a readily accessible channel for information exchange with other middle-class parents regarding magnet school curriculum, climates, racial composition, and reputation. The information gathered and shared among the social network members is richly detailed, reliable, and relevant.

Terry Bloome, a full-time mother whose husband owns a landscaping business, is a member of a closely knit, stable, and predominantly Jewish neighborhood. She pointed to the tightly interwoven neighborhood networks, including the regularity and predictability of soccer practices, as key resources for sharing information about schools:

> We are real into soccer. [These] are the kinds of parents that just talk the whole time during the soccer practice. . . . We are just always talking about the schools and what everybody is doing about magnets.

Donna Murphy, a production editor for a publishing company, explained that she knew very little about school when her daughter turned 6 years old. She consulted a neighbor:

> She is a teacher, so I trusted her judgment, even though I'm not close to her or anything. The only time I talk to her is when we talk about things like that, but I trust her judgment. I thought I was going to send [my daughter] to the neighborhood school until I talked to that woman down the street.

Donna also relies on her kinship networks, which include a sister-in-law who is a teacher in Cincinnati, and friends who are teachers in the area. This connection to "insider information" provides a referral or "frame of reference" that renders a manifest and measurable advantage to some parents. Donna explained:

> I think that is why a lot of people stick with their neighborhood schools because it is safe and they don't know that maybe sending them somewhere else would be better. They don't have that frame of reference. I'm glad I have that to influence my decisions.

Shannelle Freeman, a youth counselor with the juvenile court, served on a local advisory committee to the Cincinnati School Board a few years ago. She noted that her unique experience and position paid an invaluable dividend in terms of access to and assessment of the information she gathered. As Shannelle described the process:

> My number one [issue] was that anything was better than my neighborhood school. So my investigation was not hard for me since I was already a part of the system. A lot of parents lack [this] because they don't know what is out there. It is not a matter of being a bad parent. It is a matter of not knowing what is available and then after you find out what is available, not knowing how to critique it.

Occupations that provide broader contact with the public also provide opportunities to tap into information sources that might otherwise not be available to parents. Danetta Mitchell, a parent in St. Louis who is a beautician, learned about magnet schools for her daughter after several conversations with her customers. The information gleaned from these discussions was crucial in selecting a school, as she explained:

> One of my customers is a public school teacher. I talked with her about the international studies magnet. We have a lot of teachers that come to the shop so I got to know a little about the magnet schools. One of my customers works for the board of education and she brought me an application, so I just sent it in. . . . Most of my

friends and people I associate with, we have children and they know people and we always talk.

Lower-income Parents and the Process of School Choice

As a consequence of the relationship between social-class structure (employment, education, income) and social networks, the pool of resources from which lower-income parents can draw to make decisions regarding school-choice programs may be somewhat smaller than the one available to middle-class parents (Smrekar, 1996). This constraint is particularly evident for parents who are not employed, never finished high school or attended college, and live in Cincinnati neighborhoods that are unstable and transient, unsafe and isolated. These parents are far less likely to have friends or family members who work in the school system. In the absence of the type of social networks that can deliver relevant and valuable information regarding magnet school options, applications, and deadlines, lower-income parents tend to "luck into" the system of school choice in Cincinnati.

Consider Anne Cooke, a mother of three who rents a small two-bedroom apartment in a neighborhood about three miles from the MaSAC campus. Anne is unemployed and receives government assistance (AFDC—Aid to Families with Dependent Children). She was unaware of the curricular focus of the Math-Science Academy when she enrolled her daughter there 2 years ago. Anne opted for a magnet school because her neighborhood school "is in a terrible part of town for a 5-year-old."

Q: How did you hear about MaSAC?
A: My niece went there 3 years ago.
Q: What did you know about it before you sent your daughter there?
A: Not a lot. I just felt it was a better neighborhood and a better school to go to than where they would have had to go.

Several of the other lower-income parents were similarly vague, unclear, or uninformed regarding magnet school options and the curricular focus of their child's school. Although some of these parents are employed, they tend to work in occupations that disallow workplace associations, either by structure or by design (e.g., janitorial services, night shifts, etc.). Orleta Pierce, with two school-age sons, has a GED and works the midnight–7 A.M. shift in the housekeeping unit of a nursing home. Although Orleta has lived in Cincinnati for almost 20 years, she said she doesn't know many people. In contrast to her rural hometown in southern Kentucky, "you can't get anyone up here to help you without wanting something back."

Q: What led you to select MaSAC two years ago?

A: I used to be a school bus driver and I liked the way that they treated their children after they got out. It wasn't rowdy; it seemed like they were more in control.

Q: Does the school emphasize something special?

A: It has some special programs in there, but I don't really know what MaSAC means. I would have to ask. . . . I tell you I fell in love with this school. I really liked it from being over there. [My son] doesn't get in fights. He comes home.

Another parent, Mrs. Althea Robinson, who is a public school teacher in Cincinnati and has a son at Greenwood Paideia, provided a sketch of the parents with whom she has spoken about the magnet school program. Her view is consistent with the images drawn by lower-income parents interviewed for this study. The nature and quality of the information available to these families is markedly different from and distressingly inferior to that available to higher-income families. As Mrs. Robinson explained:

All they know is that it is an alternative program that is better than the alternative [a neighborhood school]. They don't really know what the [magnet] program is about. They just want their kid in one to keep him out of trouble or to change his environment, change his friends, that type of thing.

Chontelle Willis, a single parent of three children, works the night shift as a patient care technician at a public hospital in St. Louis. Her son, Jamal, attends Overbrook Basic Academy.

Q: What did you know about Overbrook at the time of your decision to enroll Jamal?

A: I didn't know anything. I just read one of those papers where it says the magnet programs and I filled it out. . . . My little boy, he picked the school. He is the first one that went.

Q: Why do you think he picked that one?

A: Because it said academy. He thought that it probably was going to be a military school and he wanted to wear a uniform.

Q: What do they have at Overbrook that is special?

A: I don't know. I guess it is just the change of classrooms or something, just the different way they teach. They make it more interesting than the regular school.

Although Mrs. Willis is satisfied with her choice of school, the context for this decision indicates something far less than an informed opinion or a general understanding of the options represented in the magnet school program. Our interviews with Mrs. Willis and other lower-income families in the study suggest a pattern of decision making in the context of little information or understanding about the school choice. Indeed, when these parents were asked what they knew about their school at the time of their decision, almost all said "nothing." Even when the curricular focus is distinctive and demands a particular learning and teaching style, such as the one at Greenwood Paideia in Cincinnati, parents may be less informed, at least initially, than we assume.

An important perspective is offered by two parents interviewed for the study, Van and Lativa Brown. The Browns are teachers in Cincinnati. They collected informational materials on the Paideia program prior to selecting Greenwood for their daughter. Before they mailed their application for Greenwood, they spoke with Paideia teachers in the district.

> *Q:* What is your perception of how much parents know about the Greenwood Paideia program? How much do they know about the curriculum?
>
> *Lativa:* Not a whole lot. I don't think they know much about it.
>
> *Van:* All they know is the reputation of the school. That is what most parents go by, the reputation of the school, talking to other parents. The academic program. . . . It is important to them, but they don't have much of an idea. The reputation is that it is a good school, good discipline, a place where their child can learn.

This pattern of information, knowledge, and networks in a context of school choice supports earlier research that indicates that the relative resource accounts of social networks are directly related to members' social structural position (Cochran, 1990; Cochran & Brassard, 1979; Lareau, 1989). Although personal choice shapes the pattern of all parents' social networks, these choices tend to be far more constrained for low-income families; higher-income families are more likely to be members of social networks that provide information on school processes and practices (Lareau, 1989; Smrekar, 1993). In a comprehensive review of parent information patterns in 10 Massachusetts cities involved in controlled-choice plans, Glenn (1993) concludes:

> Urban environments include low-income parents, minority parents, non-English speaking parents—groups in which many members have neither automatic access to information about schools, nor knowledge of channels for getting information. (p. 3)

DISTRICT INFORMATION DISSEMINATION

Without social networks to provide richly detailed and accurate information, lower-income families necessarily rely more heavily than do higher-income families on magnet school literature disseminated by the school district. Indeed, our survey results indicate that low-income families utilize school newsletters at a higher rate than do higher-income families. Low-income families are much less likely to visit schools than are higher-income families when considering a magnet school for their children. Only 32% of the low-income parents in magnet schools in St. Louis indicated that they visited the schools, compared with 58% of high-income parents. Similarly, in Cincinnati, higher-income parents are twice as likely to visit schools during the choice process as are low-income parents. How effective are printed materials in communicating to those families who rely on this resource for information on magnet schools in Cincinnati and St. Louis? Are dissemination strategies adequate to meet the needs of all families?

Both school districts provide information to parents on their magnet school programs. For example, the Cincinnati Public School District (CPSD) publishes annually a comprehensive guide for parents that includes one-page descriptions of each school, along with applications, school addresses, and deadline information. A magnet school brochure is mailed to the home of every student enrolled in the CPSD for whom the district has an address. In addition, the district regularly advertises on radio and television, and in the newspaper, with specific information to parents regarding the magnet school option. Still, the parents surveyed and interviewed in our study indicated that they utilize these resources at much lower rates than they do their social networks. Three factors seem to influence this pattern of utilization: the process of choosing, the source of information or "the messenger," and the quality of the information provided.

The Process of Choosing

The issue of how parents go about enrolling their children in school is illustrated by an observation offered by Verda Jackson, an executive with the Urban League and the mother of a student at MaSAC. Her comments suggest that motivation and incentive are critical dimensions of choice when districts compel only those parents who are considering an alternative to the neighborhood system of schools to file an application. As Mrs. Jackson explained:

> I know it gets in the paper, but unless there is something you are looking for, you are interested in at the time, you don't see it; it probably goes over your head.

Other controlled-choice systems, including that in Massachusetts, have abolished automatic assignment systems based on neighborhood residence. All parents must choose a school under the Massachusetts model, whether it is a neighborhood school or an alternative school.

The Source of Information

The source of information in a magnet school program is salient and problematic under conditions in which parents may be inexperienced and unfamiliar with or intimidated by schools and school people. For parents whose educational experiences were unhappy, unsuccessful, or short-lived, the idea of expanding the channels of communication with the district, the school, or an individual teacher in the process of exploring the magnet school option may represent a formidable obstacle to choice. Mrs. Jackson, a MaSAC parent, observed:

> The red tape can be daunting for people, particularly if they have not had a successful experience in school themselves. So going back and trying to deal with the school system where they don't see any positives that had come out of it for them can be very daunting for some people. [They think] "I'm just not going to do that."

The issues of familiarity and credibility are critical in this context. As another MaSAC parent suggested, "Word of mouth is probably still the best way to get information that you trust."

Again, consider the comments of Van and Lativa Brown, who are teachers in the Cincinnati Public School District with two children enrolled at Greenwood Paideia. They noted that many parents with whom they discuss the magnet school program—and most of these parents are lower-income and African American—are unfamiliar with the policies designed to enhance the accessibility of these school options. Many parents do not realize, for example, that transportation is provided to all students in the magnet program; parents need not have a car in order to apply. Mrs. Morris suggested that there are many appropriate strategies untapped by the district:

> If you want to get a lot of African American parents, you pass out information at church. Put a flyer in a grocery bag: These are the programs that are available in your district. Get where people are. Some people can't afford newspapers. Everybody doesn't watch television. There are other [ways] you can communicate.

The issue of targeted outreach is particularly relevant to Jacine Cody, a Head Start administrator and a parent of a son at Greenwood Paideia. Cody has organized a meeting between Head Start parents and a district representative for the past 4 years that is designed to introduce the magnet school option to parents who would otherwise not be aware of the program. Cincinnati school officials discontinued this practice last year, even though many of the Head Start parents interviewed for this study indicated that they would have never known about, or trusted, the idea of a magnet school for their children if not for this personal contact from the district. Cody suggested that the district could reach many hard-to-reach parents through a targeted outreach in day care centers, human services departments, and churches. The principal of Greenwood Paideia engaged in this type of targeted outreach during the initial 2 years of enrollment. The principal visited day care centers, churches, Head Start programs, and community centers to talk to parents about the new Paideia magnet school. His success in "selling the program" may be measured in the full-capacity enrollment figures registered throughout this period. Cody explained the challenges of reaching this population of parents:

> We have a lot of parents that can't read. They don't understand what is going on, so I think some extra effort needs to go into making people aware.

The Quality of Information

This issue resonated with a number of parents interviewed for this study. Recall Danetta Mitchell, the beautician in St. Louis who learned about the magnet school application process when one of her customers, a district employee, brought Danetta an application. Danetta suggested that many parents are confused and discouraged by the information disseminated by the district. Much of what they hear about the magnet schools has to do with long waiting lists. There are lots of questions and little understanding:

> You hear it on the radio but they don't give a lot of information about how to go about it. They could say, call so and so, or give information about the atmosphere of the schools or what the kids can get out of it. They don't do that.

Many of the most vocal and extensive responses were offered by parents whose professional positions provide a unique view of the relationship between information and client response; these comments focus on the need to make information clear and concise and understandable to all readers. The president of the PTO at MaSAC, Linda Jones, was succinct in her criticism of the district information mailed to school parents:

> The way they word it sometimes makes it so difficult to understand. It's like trying to read a legal paper.

Verda Jackson of the Urban League and a MaSAC parent underscored the importance of using language in all district information campaigns that is both relevant and accessible:

> I think all publicity should be developed around people who have no transportation and no telephone. How do you reach those people? It needs to be written so people can understand what they are reading. Many Head Start mothers are under 25 years old. You are dealing with someone that was not given the skills to access the system.

POLICY IMPLICATIONS

The insights offered by the parents we interviewed for this study outline a set of policy imperatives for educational leaders and policymakers. They demand that the architects and managers of magnet school systems attend to the important differences in parents' capacities to maximize choice decisions and to participate effectively and strategically in the process of choosing school options. The findings from magnet school programs in Cincinnati and St. Louis speak directly to differences among parents in their process of choosing, their sources of information, and the quality of information available to parents.

First, we believe that the process of choosing schools in a system with magnets would be enhanced under a mandatory selection system that elevates the *option* of choice to an affirmative decision or obligation. Evidence drawn from the health care sector provides dramatic documentation of the positive effect of mandatory decision making on the type, quality, and availability of information and on the "culture of choice" (Ball, 1993).

Second, we contend that the "test of equity" is perhaps nowhere more relevant than in the area of the quality of information available to parents regarding school choice options (see the Office of Educational Research and Improvement, 1992). The literacy and native language of parents are a paramount concern, as well as outlets for the dissemination of information that take account of formal and informal communication channels within various ethnic communities.

Parent information centers (PICs) like those established in the Cambridge, Massachusetts, controlled-choice program may provide a partial solution to the concern around issues of equity. There are more than 20 PICs in Boston and Cambridge and each one features:

- a convenient location near public transportation;
- three or four multiculturally representative staff/counselors on duty
- materials about local public schools, and maps showing their locations
- office hours that include evenings

The research indicates that PICs have been instrumental in providing information that is reliable, accurate, and accessible to disadvantaged and minority parents (Glenn et al., 1993). As Cookson (1994) notes: "Parent information centers are community resources that bring schools and families together and act as benign brokers of educational choice. Without investments in these centers, the process of school choice becomes chaotic, uninformed, and potentially destructive to children" (p. 136).

Although parent information centers respond to some of the equity concerns related to the source and quality of information available to parents, our research findings argue for a broader strategy, one that "taps into" the lines of trust and communication already established by existing social networks and community-based organizations, including civic and labor groups, and religious and volunteer organizations. As Petronio (1996) notes in her research on controlled choice in Cambridge, Massachusetts, parents rely heavily on social networks even in an environment in which the PIC program is well organized and well known. Thus, a strategy dependent on parent information centers is of rather limited value. The Cambridge findings as well as our data from Cincinnati and St. Louis underscore the importance of connecting with parents' social networks in order to expand channels of communication and information exchange in an environment that is considered by participants to be trustworthy and reliable. The information should be disseminated in places where parents live and do business—in grocery stores, community health centers, doctors' offices, gas stations, laundromats, churches and temples, and public housing offices. Also, the information-dissemination strategy should include a targeted outreach to those families most difficult to reach, including the most socially and residentially isolated. A diffuse information-dissemination campaign guided by persons with clout and credibility who are indigenous to the community would signal a critical degree of understanding and support to maintain a system of school choice dedicated to equity as well as to excellence.

CONCLUSION

As we noted in the introduction to this chapter, rational choice theory assumes that parents consider their personal values and their children's needs in the process of defining preferences and making choices. These preferences necessarily vary across families and are pegged to an array of differences in family backgrounds, expectations, and school experiences. Our research on magnet schools does not contest this principle of school choice. Our interest and scrutiny apply to the element of rational choice theory that is inextricably linked to parents' preferences—that is, the assumption that parents consider alternatives in the context of accurate and adequate information. Magnet school systems across the United States are grafted onto this fundamental ideal.

Our study suggests that rational choice theory is a useful lens for viewing public school choice but that the application of this theory must go beyond the narrow perspective that indicates that parents, as individuals, make rational choices isolated from their social contexts and networks. Rational choice theorists, particularly James Coleman (1990), have provided an important framework to analyze individual choice-making within a social context. Our data suggest that parents rely on others within their social networks to collect information to make choices regarding their children's education. As parents begin to share their information, interpretations, and judgments, making a choice moves from an isolated, private, or individual act to a more shared or communal process. As Goldring and Shapira (1993) note, although rational choice theory explains social phenomena influenced by individual behavior, there is a point at which individual self-interest converges with a "public" action.

This chapter underscores the value of considering the ways in which social networks provide access to the resources that are central for parents in managing and enhancing the educational choices offered by some school districts. We believe it is important to consider the degree to which design problems and program flaws affect equity issues in some school choice programs. If equity is viewed as a product of the inputs in the choice equation, the inequity found in these magnet school programs can be diminished by addressing the strengths and limitations of district- and school-level policies designed to provide accurate and accessible information to all parents regarding choice options. If we consider that one of the most compelling elements of school choice is the opportunity for parents to match their interests, preferences, and priorities with the distinctive programs offered by schools of choice, the quality of information available regarding magnet programs remains a concern.

Under conditions in which parents choose schools based on particular values and expectations, a manifest sense of membership in a value community is established (Coleman & Hoffer, 1987). A value community, which unites people around a common educational philosophy and comprises parents who are strangers from various neighborhoods, backgrounds, and occupations, is enacted through the process of choice *only* when knowledge of school standards, curriculum, and teaching contexts is equally shared among all parents. In the next chapter, we examine these issues and explore the nature of community in magnet and nonmagnet schools.

CHAPTER 4

Community or Anonymity?
Patterns of Parent Involvement
and Family–School Interactions
in Magnet Schools

Many proponents of school choice, including magnet school supporters, argue that it will result in greater parent involvement, satisfaction, empowerment, and sense of community (Bryk & Driscoll, 1988; Goldring & Shapira, 1993; Smrekar, 1996). It is also believed that family choice will lessen school bureaucracy and force schools to be more responsive to parental demands (Bryk, Lee, & Smith, 1990; Chubb & Moe, 1990; Raywid, 1989). Choice may increase communication between home and school and promote parent commitment to that school, elements that are crucial in developing a stronger sense of community and communal opportunities to learn. As Cookson (1993) notes, "Choice enables families . . . to come together in a common effort; school choice rests on social trust and if designed properly, school choice plans can build social trust" (p. 2). Advocates of school choice suggest that choice can integrate families into school communities in ways that may break down the traditional barriers that isolate schools from parents through a supportive, caring climate. Some research has indicated that schools of choice, especially Catholic schools and public magnet schools with a clear, focused mission, have higher levels of parent involvement (Bauch & Goldring, 1995; Coleman & Hoffer, 1987). Skeptics, however, contend that magnet schools may work to further the fragmentation of communities already splintered through disinvestment and forced busing strategies (Smrekar, 1996).

The home-school relationship in schools of choice is often described in terms of a communitarian model of school organization. The communitarian school organization, in contrast to a bureaucratic one, fosters a greater sense of social cohesiveness among students, parents, and school professionals. As Smrekar (1996) notes, parents are bound by a perception of shared interests and mutual goals embodied in the act of public choice. These schools, it is suggested, unlike schools within a geographic community, can develop a joint system of identity and belonging among all school members: parents, students, and professionals.

The purpose of this chapter is to explore the nature of home-school relationships in magnet schools. Although the concept of community has been explored for centuries, the linkages between community and controlled choice are primarily speculative and conceptual. As indicated, proponents of choice claim that to the degree that school choice promotes the conditions and processes that lead to the basic elements of community—commitment, communication, and collegiality—magnet schools serve a critical function in enhancing educational opportunities and experiences for students and their families (Chubb & Moe, 1990; Raywid, 1988). Some critics, however, argue that school choice will intensify stratification and alienation (Moore & Davenport, 1989).

COMMUNITY AND CHOICE: SOME THEORETICAL AND EMPIRICAL PERSPECTIVES

Contemporary concepts of community (e.g., Bronfenbrenner, Moen, & Garbarino, 1984; Coleman & Hoffer, 1987; Newmann & Oliver, 1968; Scherer, 1972; Steinberg, 1989) distinguish between a concept associated with physical or geographical boundaries and a concept of community grounded in social structures and social relations. For example, Newmann and Oliver (1968) include the following criteria in their definition, each of which is viewed as a continuum and indicative of greater or lesser degrees of community: (1) Membership is valued as an end in itself, not merely as a means to other ends; (2) members share commitment to a common purpose; and (3) members have enduring and extensive personal contact with each other. The sense of solidarity, membership, and mutual support that results from community is thought to impact the individual in terms of personal development and integration, and the larger society in terms of social cohesion and stability (Raywid, 1988).

A distinct component of the concept of community is a social network, or a social system of formal and informal organizations and opportunities for information exchange and face-to-face interactions among individuals (Cochran & Brassard, 1979; Steinberg, 1989). A social network may be defined as those individuals outside the household who engage in activities and exchanges of an affective and/or material nature with members of the immediate family (Cochran & Brassard, 1979). Members who are considered a part of a functional social network are characterized by well-known roles and contexts (neighborhood, relatives, work- or school-mates, people in agencies or organizations, etc.) and are distinguished from a more peripheral social circle (Cochran & Henderson, 1986).

Researchers have extended the concept of community by exploring the nature and stability of connections between organizations and individuals. In a comparative analysis of private and public schools, Coleman and Hoffer (1987) examined the impact of community on the degree of social integration between families and schools. The researchers asserted that the type and strength of community in schools differentially affect the critical social connections that bond families and schools in the joint enterprise of education. This concept of community refers to two types: functional and value. Functional communities are characterized by structural consistency between generations in which social norms and sanctions arise out of the social structure itself, and both reinforce and perpetuate that structure (Coleman & Hoffer, 1987). Functional communities exhibit a high degree of uniformity and cohesion within geographical, social, economic, and ideological boundaries. Value communities describe a collection of people who share similar values about education and childrearing but who are not a functional community; they are strangers from various neighborhoods, backgrounds, and occupations united around an educational organization—their children's school. The families of neighborhood school students may possess few if any of the constitutive elements of either a functional or a value community. While public neighborhood schools a century ago served residential areas that were functional communities, social and technological changes have transformed many of these communities from enclaves of shared values and daily face-to-face talk to somewhat disparate sets of interests and weak affiliations. It is certainly true, however, that some neighborhood schools, particularly those that serve middle- and upper-middle-class families who establish residence in neighborhoods with "good" schools, reflect elements of both value and functional communities. The point here is that, in general, these influences are less prevalent and less pervasive than in either public choice or nonpublic schools.

The Concept of School as a Community

The vision of the school as a community portrays adults and students linked to one another by a common mission and by a network of supportive personal relations that strengthen their commitment to the organization (Bryk & Driscoll, 1988). Three core components construct this communal school organization (Bryk & Driscoll, 1988): (1) a system of shared values among members of the organization that includes the "norms of schooling" (Bird & Little, 1986): norms for instruction, which affect the way teachers' work is conducted and student learning takes place; and norms for civility, which affect the relations among individuals in the institution; (2) a common agenda of activities, which includes those formal and informal events that enable school participants to engage in face-to-face interactions, promote social ties, and encourage communal associations; and (3) a pattern of social relations that embodies collaboration and extensive involvement and is highlighted by the collegiality shared among the adults in the school and the expanded role of the teacher.

Driscoll (1995) notes that community develops from a context in which individuals derive meaning:

> This concept of school community reflects the needs that are derived from shared activities and territory but also embodies the culture of sentiments, traditions, and practices that link its members and from which they take meaning. Community is neither spontaneous nor passive; it is derived from a living memory and is both created and nurtured by its members. (p. 220)

Home-School Relationships in Schools of Choice: Indicators of Community

The research on the dynamic intersection of community and choice is primarily speculative and conceptual. Although much empirical research has been conducted on home-school relationships in general, only limited research has focused on home-school relationships in schools of choice. In fact, much of the literature on school choice and parental involvement is emerging as two, separate discourses (see Bauch & Goldring, 1995). Research that has been conducted has focused on parent satisfaction with schools of choice, rather than patterns of involvement, communication, and commitment (Driscoll, 1991; Witte, 1996).

A common theme in the limited empirical research is that parental involvement is heightened in schools where parents have made a choice. For example, Witte (1996) reports that parents who participate in the Milwaukee voucher experiment are more involved in their "schools of choice" than they were in the public schools. Parents who participated in the public school choice system in San Antonio (Martinez, Thomas, & Kemerer, 1996) also were more highly involved in schools than were nonchoice parents.

Others have hypothesized about the relationship between choice and involvement. Bryk and colleagues (1990), for example, have reported on the effects of high school organization on teachers, students, and parents. They argue that parental choice can result in a more democratic organizational context that supports involvement, commitment, and trust. Bauch and Goldring (1995) found that schools of choice such as Catholic schools and single-focus magnet schools that have a unified mission and curricular focus appear better able to provide opportunities for parental involvement and effective communication between home and schools. Others suggest that in choosing schools, it is expected that parents might exercise influence in schools in an attempt to effect change (cf. Bauch & Goldring, 1998; Hirschman, 1970). However, evidence that parents in schools of choice have the capacity to influence decisions is thin (Malen, 1994). Others suggest that parents may make an initial choice of a school and then delegate responsibility to the school for their child's education, exempting their own involvement (Bauch, 1989).

The purpose of this chapter is to "bring community back" into the discussion about school choice and families. While conceptual work on school choice suggests that choice is a powerful engine for creating the constitutive elements of community, this study provides both survey and ethnographic data that examine the nature and extent of these relationships.

We focus on six areas of home-school relationships: (1) level of parent involvement at school, (2) amount of parent influence on school policies, (3) amount of parent-parent interactions outside of school, (4) amount of information the school provides to parents, (5) frequency of teacher communication with parents, and (6) the extent to which the school has a caring, supportive school climate in which parents feel welcome.[1] Means and standard deviations for the survey responses and ethnographic data are shown in Table 4.1. We begin by exploring parents' perceptions of home-school relationships and school community, and follow this discussion with teachers' views on parental participation and parent-teacher communication.

SCHOOL COMMUNITY IN MAGNET AND NONMAGNET SCHOOLS

Parent Perspectives

The survey data from the parent questionnaires reveal that, overall, parents report low levels of school community in all schools. Parents are only rarely or sometimes involved in school activities. Only 35% of Cincinnati magnet school parents and 28% of nonmagnet parents report that they often attend school meetings and parent-teacher conferences. Parents also indicate that they have very little influence in school decision making. When asked how much influence they had, for example, in setting school goals, only 8% of magnet parents in St. Louis and 15% of nonmagnet parents said

Table 4.1 Definition of School Community Variables

		Cincinnati		St. Louis	
Variables	*Measures*	Mean	(S.D.)	Mean	(S.D.)
Parent Background Characteristics					
Income	9-point scale from <$7,500 (1) to >$100,000 (9)	39.0*	(38.2)	21.7*	(21.3)
Ethnicity	African American = 1; White = 0	0.51	(0.50)	0.70	(0.46)
School Community	*4-Point Scales:*				
1. Parent Involve-ment at School	from never (1) to often (4)	2.28	(0.73)	2.39	(0.63)
2. Parent Influence	from none (1) to a great deal (4)	2.17	(0.72)	2.05	(0.73)
3. Parent-Parent Interaction	from never (1) to often (4)	1.74	(0.63)	1.59	(0.58)
4. School Informa-tion to Parents	from never (1) to often (4)	2.44	(0.56)	2.32	(0.56)
5. Teacher Communi-cation with Parents	from never (1) to many times (4)	2.36	(0.90)	2.44	(0.93)
6. Supportive School Climate	from strongly disagree (1) to strongly agree (4)	3.04	(0.56)	3.07	(0.46)

*In thousand dollars, estimated from midpoints of relevant intervals
Data: Self-Reports from Parent Surveys; *see* Appendix B

they had a great deal of influence. Parents also indicate that they rarely have contact with other parents. On average, only about 10% of all parents interact frequently with other parents at school events. Furthermore, parents also report that they rarely or only sometimes receive information about the school, and have occasional communications from their children's teachers. Only about 25% of the parents in both magnet and nonmagnet schools receive information on a regular basis about learning tips for their children. In sum, parents in both magnet and nonmagnet schools are not reporting very intensive interactions with their children's schools or teachers. There is one exception: All parents, but especially magnet school parents, perceive a very caring, supportive climate where they feel comfortable and safe. Close to 50% of magnet school parents in both Cincinnati and St. Louis indicate they feel comfortable spending time at their child's school.

Despite the generally low levels of home-school connections and school community, are there differences in the frequency of contact among parents and teachers in magnet and nonmagnet schools?[2] We turn first to Cincinnati. Controlling for differences in the socioeconomic background of parents, analysis of the parent questionnaires suggests that magnet and nonmagnet schools differ in the nature of the home-school relations (see Table 4.2). More magnet school parents report a supportive, caring climate that welcomes parental involvement than do nonmagnet school parents. In addition, magnet school parents are more involved in their children's school and report receiving more frequent information about the school than do nonmagnet parents. In contrast, nonmagnet school parents report that they have more interactions with parents and more communication with teachers than do magnet school parents. There is no difference between magnet and nonmagnet schools in levels of parental influence.

In St. Louis, as in Cincinnati, our survey data indicate that magnet school parents are more involved at school than are nonmagnet parents (see Table 4.2). In addition, more magnet parents report a caring, supportive school climate than do nonmagnet parents. However, nonmagnet parents in St. Louis interact with other parents more frequently and receive more communication from their child's teachers than do magnet school parents.

Interestingly, nonintegrated nonmagnet schools stand out among magnet and integrated nonmagnet school in several categories. Compared with magnet and integrated nonmagnet schools, nonintegrated school parents report greater influence on decision making and more parent-parent interactions. Similarly, the nonintegrated school parents report that the school

Table 4.2 Means and Standard Deviations (in parentheses) of School Community Variables According to Choice Arrangement

	Cincinnati		St. Louis		
				Nonmagnet	
Parents' Perspectives	Magnet (N = 353)	Nonmagnet (N = 361)	Magnet (N = 483)	Integrated (N = 256)	Nonintegrated (N = 214)
1. Parent Involvement at School	2.46 (0.70)	2.10 (0.73)	2.46 (0.60)	2.23 (0.64)	2.41 (0.66)
2. Parent Influence	2.24 (0.71)	2.10 (0.73)	2.04 (0.68)	1.99 (0.77)	2.13 (0.81)
3. Parent-Parent Interaction	1.78 (0.67)	1.69 (0.60)	1.50 (0.53)	1.62 (0.61)	1.80 (0.62)
4. School Information to Parents	2.54 (0.56)	2.34 (0.55)	2.32 (0.53)	2.31 (0.61)	2.36 (0.60)
5. Teacher Communication with Parents	2.42 (0.90)	2.31 (0.90)	2.31 (0.92)	2.44 (0.95)	2.75 (0.88)
6. Supportive School Climate	3.19 (0.49)	2.88 (0.60)	3.15 (0.41)	2.97 (0.52)	3.01 (0.49)

provides somewhat more information about the school than do the other school types, and there is greater teacher communication with parents.

In both Cincinnati and St. Louis, parents report relatively low levels of family-school interactions. After controlling for income and ethnicity, the findings suggest that there is more parent involvement in magnet schools than in nonmagnet schools, with the exception of the nonintegrated nonmagnet schools in St. Louis, which are similar to magnet schools in many ways. Parents in magnet schools and the nonintegrated schools in St. Louis report attending more school activities, volunteering more frequently, and coming to school more often to discuss problems. Magnet schools in both districts excel in providing parents with a sense that they are welcome, and in developing a caring, supportive school climate. This finding supports the idea that parents who choose a school often perceive they are part of a school community that is marked with unity of purpose and social cohesion (Smrekar, 1996).

Teacher Perspectives

In our survey research we asked teachers in both magnet and nonmagnet schools about communicating, interacting with, and involving parents (see Figure 4.1 & 4.2). In both Cincinnati and St. Louis, the overall levels of teacher outreach to parents are extremely low. Teachers rarely contact parents, almost never engage with them about educational activities in the home, and rarely interact with parents at nonschool community events. All teachers indicate rather low levels of parental involvement in the schools, although, consistent with parent reports, magnet school teachers report slightly higher levels of parental involvement. There are no differences between magnet and nonmagnet school teachers in the extent to which they contact parents about such issues as volunteering in the classroom, assisting on field trips, and attending school meetings and conferences. Similarly, teachers in both magnet and nonmagnet schools almost never interact with parents at nonschool events such as local church and community programs. It should be noted that teachers in nonintegrated nonmagnet schools seem to be communicating and interacting with parents more than teachers in integrated nonmagnet schools in St. Louis. (For a complete discussion of nonintegrated nonmagnet schools in St. Louis, see Morris, 1997.)

Importantly, despite the low levels of home-school communication, the survey data indicate that nonmagnet school teachers communicate more frequently than their magnet counterparts about a specific issue: how parents can help their children at home. Nonmagnet teachers may perceive this activity differently due to the lower socioeconomic backgrounds of most of their students.

Figure 4.1 Teacher Reports About Amount of Home-School Involvement in Cincinnati

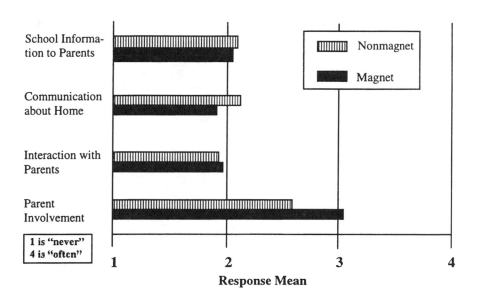

Figure 4.2 Teacher Reports About Amount of Home-School Involvement in St. Louis

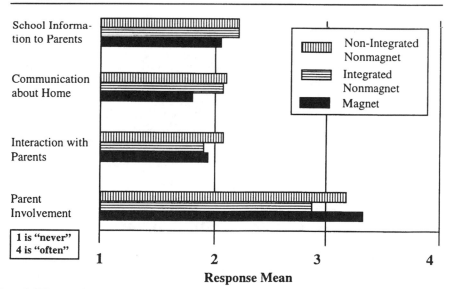

Data: Self-Reports from Teacher Surveys; *see* Appendix B.

We surveyed teachers regarding possible barriers to parental involvement. Not surprisingly, magnet school teachers are significantly more likely than nonmagnet teachers to indicate that distance and travel are barriers to parental involvement. Forty percent of magnet school teachers, compared with 14% of nonmagnet teachers, indicated that transportation was a barrier to parental involvement in St. Louis. In addition, magnet teachers are significantly more likely to indicate that parents' work schedules are a barrier to parental involvement than are nonmagnet teachers. In contrast, nonmagnet teachers are significantly more likely to indicate parental apathy as a barrier to parental involvement. For example, in Cincinnati, 50.3% of the nonmagnet teachers compared with only 17.8% of the magnet teachers indicated that parental apathy often affects parental involvement in the schools.

Teachers in magnet schools acknowledge the unique circumstances of parents that can make ongoing communication and involvement difficult. They seem to understand that transportation and work schedules make it hard for parents to come to school for events, conferences, or volunteer activities. This pattern of distance and disconnection, however, suggests that teachers are not experimenting with alternative strategies to overcome these barriers, nor are they enhancing traditional means of communication to try to compensate for the difficulties of promoting face-to-face interactions. We did not see evidence of parent-teacher conferences scheduled in alternative (community-based) sites, or of home visits and other nontraditional parent outreach. The status quo continues. Nonmagnet teachers attempt to communicate more frequently with parents, but they also tend to have a stereotypical view of many parents: Parents do not come to school because they do not care.

Magnet schools have been promoted as opportunities to bring schools and parents closer together: Parents choose schools; they will be more involved; teachers and parents have a shared purpose and missions for the children that can result in closer home-school ties. These possible benefits of school choice cannot materialize without clear, concerted efforts to "bring the community back in" (Smrekar, 1996). The next section further illuminates the perspectives of parents and teachers regarding efforts to link schools and families.

COMMUNITIES OF SHARED VALUES

The elements of value consistency and congruency critical to a foundation of school community were expressed in strong and vivid terms by magnet school parents during lengthy interviews (see Appendix A for full descriptions of the magnet schools in the study). The exercise of choice represented in a magnet school selection provides a manifest sense of union and membership among these widely scattered, geographically distant families. These parents think of themselves as separate and distinct from other "public" school parents; to them, their choice represents a significant break from the pervasive elements of compromise and complacency found in "neighborhood" schools. Althea Robinson, a public school teacher and a parent of a daughter at Greenwood Paideia in Cincinnati, underscored these points:

> Everybody has a common goal, a common mission. We have one thing that we try to push for—we try to better our children through this program. We want to make sure that this program does everything that it is capable of doing.

Despite the dispersion of school families across city neighborhoods, parents perceive a communal bond. Mrs. Robinson echoed other Paideia parents with the observation:

> When you have a new program, the parents have bought into the program. And if they buy into the program, they'll work for the program. . . . When you have a staff that is supportive of the program and parents who are supportive of the program, it is bound to work.

Many parents described "the personal touch that a lot of other schools don't have" when they referred to their magnet school. John and Amanda Raffton described the familiarity that they and other families enjoy with the school staff at Overbrook Basic Academy in St. Louis—an attribute they said was missing in the neighborhood school their daughter attended before enrolling at Overbrook. Mrs. Raffton, a full-time homemaker, noted:

> The teachers are all so friendly. When I first walked into Overbrook . . . they would stop and say good morning. You get a warm welcome when you walk into that school.

The interviews with magnet school parents indicated shared perceptions of social cohesion and common purpose. Sybril Jackson, a parent at Greenwood Paideia in Cincinnati, is unemployed; she learned about the magnet program when district officials visited her son's Head Start program:

> I can truly say over my lifetime, I think this is a more close-knit school family and parents and principal than I've ever seen. . . .
> There is just something there that everybody is happy and delighted

with what is going on in your school, the same vibes. The secretary is
wonderful. The parents, when they come in, they are wonderful.

Another Greenwood parent described "a real sense of community" among
children and parents "who feel proud of the school and feel of part of it."
These conditions help sustain a sense of loyalty, membership, and involvement. Ted McGill, who has a daughter at Greenwood Paideia, described
the magnet schools as Cincinnati's "private school district" and the alternatives as the "ho-hum neighborhood schools," because "you have parents
who care at [magnet] schools." Mr. McGill, who is a satellite television technician, framed the concept of school community and variable degrees of
commitment this way:

> If you want to call it community—what is inside the school—I think
> there is something there that unites people versus, maybe, it is
> because they feel like they strive for the same goal and that everyone
> has their kids there for a particular purpose versus these other
> alternatives. Maybe that is what it is.

Against the backdrop of "public" schools (nonmagnet or neighborhood schools), parents in magnet schools construe a deeper level of commitment, caring, and trust in their school environment. The neighborhood schools are portrayed by magnet parents as places where parents
have given in to complacency and teachers have given up on standards of
academic excellence and order. Although an extensive discussion of the
topic is beyond the scope of this chapter, it is relevant here to underscore
parents' perceptions regarding some of these concrete differences between the magnets and neighborhood schools. As one Mathematics and
Science Academy of Cincinnati (MaSAC) parent put it simply, "The magnets have better textbooks, AV stuff, the doors work, the desks stay together and the outside doors don't have to be chained." The neighborhood schools, as outlined by magnet parents, are chaotic places that are
unsafe, overcrowded, and uninviting.

Our case study data suggest that the traditions and school practices
from which magnet school parents derive enriched meaning and value comprise a mythology of "specialness" associated with magnet school systems.
The myth of extra effort and extraordinary measures is best understood in
a context of urban school environments nested within communities marked
by isolation, instability, and uncertainty (see Yu & Taylor, 1997). In this light,
magnet school communities remake into something special and extraordinary the rather common and ordinary expectations related to institutional
responsiveness and professional responsibility. For example, a parent described the staff at Greenwood Paideia as "teachers who are always smiling

and talking to the kids," and a staff who "seem to enjoy being there; it is not just a job." Joyce Blewett, a mother of two children at Overbrook Basic Academy in St. Louis who works full-time as a meat-packing clerk, captured this consensus view:

> Q: What is the best part of the school program?
> A: I like the way they do things. If there is a problem, you hear about it. The principal or teacher will call you and let you know what is going on. If they are slowing down in a subject, they will tell you. If they need extra help, they keep in touch with you and let you know what is going on.

Ted McGill (whose wife works the 3:00–11:30 P.M. shift as a licensed practical nurse at the local hospital) described his interactions with the staff at Greenwood Paideia similarly, using a template that many would argue describes "the way schools ought to be."

> I think Greenwood is a good school, but I think it is the way schools should be. . . . I don't know if better [than neighborhood schools] is the word. Everyone takes their job seriously. Just the fact that I can write a note in the plan book and someone will write a note back or call me or if I say, "let's have a conference," that person asks me what my schedule is and what will work good for me. They are willing to work with you and be flexible. Where up there [neighborhood school], I had 15 minutes before school starts and 15 minutes after school ends.

Skeptics may suggest that these results point to a self-fulfilling prophecy. "It is generally assumed parents who invest in their child's education by actively making a choice will view their schools favorably. Even if there are no visible reasons for the choice to lead to satisfaction, many parents may justify their choice and investment by indicating satisfaction with the school and viewing it through 'rose colored glasses'" (Goldring & Shapira, 1993, p. 398). This argument points out that when there is an investment associated with making a choice, whether it be time, energy, or other ancillary issues, parents tend to report higher levels of school satisfaction.

Nature and Quality of Social Interactions Among Parents in Magnet Schools

The magnet school program is anchored to a set of assumptions regarding distance, desegregation, and busing, and each of these involves a set of trade-offs that may limit parent interactions: the creation of some racially balanced schools in exchange for an entire system of neighborhood schools; promotion of value communities in lieu of geographical communities; a fleet of yellow buses in place of a scattering of carpool parents, children, and "walkers." A particularly critical influence on the nature of social interactions among parents in magnets rests with the vast transportation arrangement that collects students from widely scattered city neighborhoods—many of these are racially and ethnically segregated—and deposits them at another location—a magnet school.

When the bell that signals dismissal rings each school day for the magnet school students at Overbrook Basic Academy and Viking Basic Academy in St. Louis, and Greenwood Paideia and MaSAC in Cincinnati, there are a dozen or more yellow buses and vans lined up outside the school yard gate with their engines idling. A cadre of teachers armed with clipboards, rosters, and walkie-talkies directs hundreds of children out of the building and into the waiting vehicles. Several cars and mini-vans drive into the lot and each collects a handful of students, but there is no lingering, no stopping; these are not occasions for friendly, spontaneous information sharing among parents or between school staff and the children's families. In a school environment comprised of families who live in different neighborhoods and share few social networks, these arrangements constrict opportunities for face-to-face talk that may be sustained in a geographical community (and may arise naturally in a neighborhood school). The patterns of involvement evidenced in the magnet schools reflect strong participation among parents, to be sure. The robust sense of familiarity, social cohesion, and connection that would be expected and predicted in these magnet school settings, however, is largely absent (see Smrekar, 1996).

The portraits drawn by parents in the magnet schools outline a sharp impression of commitment and caring, as noted earlier. But the lack of "shared space" among parents isolated and scattered across city neighborhoods and within family and school social structures that delimit interactions among parents to brief and unrelated episodes raises troubling doubts among many parents regarding their school "community." Terry Bloome, a stay-at-home mother of a third-grader at Greenwood Paideia, offered a response echoed by many when asked if there was a sense of community at Greenwood:

> I think when something is going on at the school, a lot of people participate, no matter what, just because it is the school and your kids go and you are going to help out. I don't think it is any more than that.

Julie Anderson, a marketing research analyst, agreed that the quality of social cohesion among parents at Greenwood is somewhat thin and tenuous. Ironically, Mrs. Anderson's base of comparison is her daughter's former school, a neighborhood elementary school that served as a gathering place for nonschool, service-related activities within the geographical community:

> I don't think I'm there enough to feel that. I did at Woodbridge [a neighborhood school] but I was at Woodbridge more because my Girl Scout troop met there after school. I can't say I feel a sense of community.

When Mrs. Anderson was asked whether parents at Greenwood are similar to her and her family, she hesitated and voiced some uncertainty:

> I think so, and there again, it ranges. I can't say I've met a lot of the parents. We've done a couple of things at school like Fun Day, and two years ago, the Halloween dance. The parents are basically from all over the community. . . . It is really spread out.

Other magnet school parents reiterated the impression of strong parent participation at school events by noting that it is often difficult to find a parking space in the lot—an inconvenience most had not experienced in their neighborhood schools. Still, parents know one another in only specific (school-based) and vague and unfamiliar ways. Consider these illuminating perspectives. Joyce Blewett, a meat-packing clerk with a child at Overbrook, noted that most parents work outside the home; this fact makes attendance at school-based events very difficult and somewhat rare:

> Q: Do you know the other parents who send their children here?
> A: No. I sit and talk to them while waiting to talk to the teachers, but I don't know them real well.
> Q: Is there a sense of community at Overbrook?
> A: You really don't create a sense of community. As far as the parents, unless the kids start running with one of the other children and you meet the parents through that way. Otherwise, there is not much of a chance to really talk or meet the other parents.

Many parents described a sense of disconnection and isolation due to hectic work schedules. Kendra Parker, who works part-time as a computer technician, offered this assessment when asked how she met other Overbrook parents:

> When we go on field trips and stuff, you meet them. They'll have parent-teacher meetings, but you really don't get to know anybody that well. I would say mostly on field trips and things, and then a lot of parents don't get to go on field trips because a lot of parents work.

Overbrook parents noted that family and work obligations limit their involvement and participation in school-based events. Except for the notable and predictable—parent meetings, open house, and the carnival fundraiser—parents rarely visit the school campus. In the absence of other linking social events, networks, or institutions, there is little familiarity among families.

Other magnet school parents responded similarly to the question of school community and social cohesion; this response from Ruby Fox, a Greenwood Paideia mother with a daughter in the fourth grade, typifies a common pattern of disconnection and anonymity:

> I only know other parents from school functions. I see people and I know them by face, but then I have to ask their name again and we kind of reintroduce ourselves just because you don't see them every day.

When asked if she tended to see the same parents at the school functions, her response was, "I would say so."

At the Mathematics and Science Academy of Cincinnati, the parents were universally vocal about the superficial quality of their interactions with other parents. The combined impact of inflexible work schedules and compressed family obligations leaves little room for involvement at school. Donna Murphy, the editorial/production assistant with a daughter at MaSAC, expressed a mixture of frustration and regret when she was asked if she knew many of the other parents at MaSAC:

> No, I don't. I really don't know any of them except one who happens to be a friend of my sister's. I work and I don't get involved with PTO. I'm a single parent and I can't do field trips and that kind of stuff.

In addition to issues of work, family, and personal responsibilities, there are more tractable elements that influence the social interactions evidenced in magnet schools. Without question, widespread busing and "neighborhood dispersion" are central influences on the abbreviated and anonymous nature of interactions among parents at the magnets. The vast majority of magnet school parents interviewed for this study said simply, "I don't know anybody there." Consider the viewpoints of Linda Jones, a nurse who works part-time, and Alma Patterson, a part-time community college student. These two mothers co-chair the PTO at MaSAC in Cincinnati.

> *Q:* How do you create a sense of community here?
> *Jones:* You can't.
> *Patterson:* There is a problem to get PTO together.
> *Jones:* That is the problem we are having. It is very hard. When you are coming from so far away and I have to say that most of our parents have to take buses; it is too long on a bus. If they do have a car, most of the time, the car is not reliable. . . . The only time we get parents here is when we offer free food.

John Raffton, an electrician and a parent of two children at Overbrook Basic Academy in St. Louis, underscored the problem of physical distances and social disconnection.

> This is one of the drawbacks of the magnet school system. You are not in the community itself. I know from my own personal experi ence. Matthew went to his first two years of grade school at Spencer [a neighborhood school]. It was only three blocks up the road. It was nothing to walk up there to find out what is going on or to help out in a school activity. But now at Overbrook, it seems so far away. It is 20 extra minutes to drive out there. A lot of times it isn't worth my time because by the time I drive out there, the activity is already halfway through.

The challenges provoked by the problems of distance and disconnection are well understood by both parents and teachers in the magnet schools. Within a school-choice policy environment that predicts new and expanded pathways for parental involvement, these issues would seemingly provoke innovative strategies to reconstitute new communities within this pattern of geographical dispersion and social dislocation. Instead, the magnet schools in Cincinnati and St. Louis have institutionalized standard communication channels (e.g., newsletters) and traditional avenues for participation in magnet schools. These include the common repertoire of parent-involvement activities: PTO meetings, fundraisers, science fairs, and holiday pageants. Parents' beliefs regarding common values and shared beliefs are tethered to these rather brief, abbreviated, and anonymous parent-to-parent interactions. There is an elevated sense of "shared meanings" that transcends a notable absence of "shared space" (Driscoll, 1995). These parents report that they "do not know many other parents" in their magnet school, but most maintain an unwavering belief that other magnet school parents are like-minded in terms of educational values, beliefs, and commitment. A consensus view among magnet parents highlights the fact that scarce discretionary time, long distances, a lack of transportation, and multiple work/family obligations interfere with their involvement in school-based activities beyond the occasional "open house" event, fundraiser, or springtime choral pageant. This suggests that most parents are like Emily Drake at Greenwood, who confided, "I can't say I've met a lot of parents." This observation was echoed by most magnet parents, with the exception of Linda Jones, who works at MaSAC as a parent volunteer coordinator. To be sure, these are communities formed around faith in an organization, not on familiarity with other members. When asked if parents at the school share common educational values, a single mother of two young boys at Overbrook Basic Academy in St. Louis reflected on the fact that there are relatively few and infrequent occasions for regular, sustained, face-to-face contact with other parents and responded, "I hope so."

Community and Anonymity: Teachers' Views

Magnet school teachers confirm the standard set of organizational arrangements designed to involve parents in the traditional set of supportive and celebratory events at their schools; they share parents' impressions of common goals and shared purposes and they lament the family stressors and structures—work lives, single-parent households, lack of transportation— that help sustain the social distance among parents and the physical distance between parents and schools. These arrangements form the basis for understanding and compromise in the magnet school system. They lead to a set of contradictions anchored to parents' tangible investment and involvement in choice, on the one hand, and a corresponding drift toward devolution and detachment in schooling, on the other. These contradictions form the crosshairs in the contest between community and anonymity in these choice arrangements.

The empowering qualities of choice were affirmed by those teachers who noted that when parents are given the opportunity to choose among magnet offerings and nonmagnet schools, parents tend to be more motivated, more involved, and more interested in that choice. Many of the magnet school teachers in Cincinnati and St. Louis are experienced educators with professional backgrounds that include teaching in neighborhood (nonmagnet) schools. They often referred to those experiences as a template against which to measure the nature and quality of family-school interactions and school community in their current school assignments. Consistent with the parents' perceptions noted earlier, these comparisons of magnets and neighborhood schools render a portrait of contrasting conditions characterized by qualities of community more manifest in the magnets. A second-grade teacher in Cincinnati's Greenwood Paideia school offered a blunt assessment of the motivation and investment evidenced in magnet school parents—qualities that are often absent, she argued, in parents whose children attend a neighborhood school in the city:

> In that [downtown] school, if I had any problem with the kids, that was my problem. It was for me to take care of. They didn't want to be bothered. But here, I see it being totally different because they want their kids to go here. They have chosen the school and they want their kids to succeed. . . . They are quite willing to talk and to discuss; they are anxious to.

Other teachers echoed the claims of choice advocates by suggesting that the mere act of choosing a school engenders an enhanced degree of commitment that pays dividends to all—parents, teachers, and students. The rewards are measured in terms of cooperation and participation in children's learning. There are assumptions here regarding a process of choosing that is thoughtful and planful, based on reliable and trustworthy information. The act of choosing moves the act of schooling from a default arrangement to an active decision-making context. A fourth-grade teacher at Overbrook Basic Academy in St. Louis summed up this enthusiastic, pro-choice viewpoint:

> I think because parents have to sign their kids up, they have to want them to go there. They don't just send them off to school because they have to send them to school. So I think you have more committed parents.

The assistant principal/instructional coordinator at Overbrook, Mrs. Travis, a veteran of 23 years in the St. Louis public schools, noted that many of their magnet parents are not "perfect"; many are poor, young, and addicted to drugs. Many are single parents. In some of these homes, according to school authorities, children have suffered sexual and physical abuse and neglect. Many of these parents live with their children in neighborhoods that crackle with the sound of gunfire at night; some are eyewitnesses to murder. "We attract anyone," she told us, "but the persons we attract are usually parents of children who want their kids to get a better education." This is the social contract parents share with magnet school teachers. It is sustained by a shared discourse and a modest faith in the system, and threatened by repeated disappointment and creeping cynicism.

Detachment and Devolution. Does the commonality expressed in shared goals among magnet school parents promote parent involvement? Not exactly. Our case studies strongly suggest that magnet school parents share a collective disposition toward devolution of responsibility in conjunction with their affirmative choice-making. The teachers in our study outlined a process in which parents' faith in the goodness of their choice results in a deference to educators in some of the key responsibilities for student learning. The detachment signals a critical rift in the relatively seamless and uncontested congruency and collaboration between educators and parents in magnet schools. The issue here is not one of apathy or disinterest among parents from the point of view of teachers; rather, the currency found in the act of choosing and the general confidence expressed in magnet schools combine to create uneven and unremarkable patterns of parental participation. In sum, the conditions are not ideal nor what some would predict when it comes to patterns of family-school interactions in magnet schools.

Teachers were blunt and unsentimental in their criticism of parents who are not involved in their children's schooling. There was little animosity expressed, mostly disappointment and creeping disillusionment with parents who seem physically and emotionally detached. A perspective offered by a veteran teacher-coach at Greenwood Paideia reflects many of his colleagues' perceptions of parents' accounting for (or rationalization of) their detachment and deference. "They see this school as a benefit and say, 'Okay, I got him in there, now you do something with him.' " The teacher-coach continued with this observation:

> A lot of parents think that I've done my dues. I've worked hard.
> I've gotten my kids into your school; now they are yours. I guess
> that is one of our pet peeves. We don't believe that parents are
> taking responsibility for raising their children. They are expecting
> us to do it.

The lack of involvement is measured in a variety of ways: poor turnout at PTO meetings and parent-teacher conferences; unreturned telephone calls; unfocused and inconsistent attention to learning problems and homework assignments. Only a core group of parents maintains a steady and reliable presence in the PTO. Others attend school-based events only when their children are performing. Volunteering is limited to a few who are able and interested. It is not what the teachers expected. The differences in parents' and teachers' expectations for involvement have provoked teachers to rethink their assumptions about parents' reasons for choosing and the information parents use in making their selections. As one teacher concluded after several years at Greenwood Paideia:

These parents might be down here because of the reputation and maybe nothing else. They know that their child is probably going to be safe here. But then it is almost like the parents wash their hands of everything else once they have gotten their child in. That is what I tend to see.

In addition to noting a lack of involvement and cooperation, teachers expressed disappointment at the contentious elements of their relationships with parents. These unpredictable and unwelcome conversations with parents lead many magnet teachers to believe that the differences between the magnets and nonmagnets, in terms of family-school relations, are slowly eroding as their interactions with more and more magnet school parents grow in intensity and hostility. As one teacher from Viking Basic School in St. Louis suggested:

If we had parent participation like we needed, this school would be perfect. If parents were made to sign a contract or something saying that they were willing to cooperate with the teacher in the school and that the teacher is not the enemy, it would be so much better.

Social and Geographical Distance. Beyond an outline of the elements of choice-making that may lead to decreased involvement in children's learning environments, magnet school teachers expressed deep concerns regarding the seemingly intractable issues of family structures and stressors that lead many families away from school involvement. Single-parent or two-parent working families—and the overwhelming majority of magnet school families fit one of these two categories—create a set of demands that often leave little room for PTO meetings, family math workshops, or volunteer fundraisers. Many parents, unable to afford a car, do not have transportation to school and must rely on public transportation—an often unreliable and unsafe alternative.

These issues are exacerbated by the fact that magnet school programs draw students from disparate neighborhoods scattered across the cities of St. Louis and Cincinnati. This physical distance translates into a perception of social distance that the magnets struggle to overcome. For the most part, too, the magnets rely on standardized volunteer mechanisms and episodic communication strategies—quarterly PTO meetings, the annual fall candy sale fundraiser, a parent-teacher conference in October, and an occasional letter home, in a context that is unlike a traditional neighborhood school arrangement in terms of physical and social distances. This pattern of communication and participation is in sharp contrast to some magnet schools across the nation that have adopted what some would consider extraordinary measures to attract the typical "estranged" magnet parent. These more aggressive parent-involvement measures include family "VIP" centers (a room at the school), regular monthly newsletters, "open-door" school visiting policies, required parent participation hours, parent-to-parent telephone trees, and contracts that specify the types of involvement activities that are expected of all parents (Smrekar, 1996).

Only MaSAC in St. Louis has responded with an innovation designed to bring parents into the school, despite the distance. MaSAC reconfigured their back-to-school night as a picnic-barbecue on the school lawn, rescheduled it in the late afternoon–early evening, and included music, balloons, and all the food. Afterward, parents are invited inside the building for a discussion of the school year with faculty and staff. MaSAC also has space set aside in the school building for a family resource center that offers GED and parenting classes, social activities, and information on child care, employment training, and other community services. Still, large groups of parents are a rarity at MaSAC and the other magnets. Only the parents who live closest to the school, who think of the magnet as their neighborhood school, regularly attend school events. "We draw from all over the city and we are not a neighborhood school," the counselor at MaSAC underscored. This means lower-than-hoped-for attendance at many of the workshops she organizes for parents. Her colleague, a second-grade teacher, described the challenges many parents encounter when they consider making a trip to the magnet school, which may be far from their neighborhood. The costs and the consequences are these:

> The parents don't have transportation. If we draw from nine different neighborhoods, we have a problem if they don't have transportation and the buses only take you so far and only run so late. I don't know too many parents who want to spend an hour and a half on a bus to get here to talk to their child's teacher, especially if it is going to be something unpleasant.

A teacher from Greenwood Paideia described the core group of "active" parents as locals from the school's surrounding neighborhood, adding, "I don't see parents coming from downtown or the opposite side of town; they have the least amount of contact with the school."

Mrs. Travis, the assistant principal at Overbrook Basic Academy, recounted the exhaustive efforts undertaken to "get parents in the school." Despite what she called "a spirit of cooperation" among the magnet school parents, this advantage is overwhelmed by the fact that Overbrook is so far away from the homes of many parents; they "have no idea where it is."

The burden of busing, distance, and social dispersion weighs heavily on the faculties and staffs of the magnets, and consumes their energy and focus on strategies designed to "bring parents in." Mrs. Travis described her frustration:

> The disadvantage of busing—if you are in the neighborhoods, you can easily get to school. You know how to get to school, for one thing. It is not as hard to get to school because you know where the school is. But here, if I'm having a parent workshop, many are going to get lost on the way. Some aren't going to come. I usually send out five or six notices. I notify everybody. If you are interested, send back the sign-up sheet. I may get back 40 sheets. I send them a notice every 5 days, and just before [the workshop], I send a note home. If I have a telephone number, I'll call them. I might be expecting 20 parents; I might get two.

The contradictions that parents in magnet schools describe—the perception of shared values and constitutive communities, despite social distance and anonymity among parents—reemerge as central themes in the teacher studies. With the exception of Greenwood Paideia, where soccer and scouting provide common links among families from widely scattered city neighborhoods, there is little in terms of familiarity, regular and sustained communication, or the "shared space" that Driscoll (1995) calls for in a robust school community. Echoing the words of the parents, magnet school teachers described an absence of contact among parents at the school and few overlapping social networks. "I don't think too many of them know each other from any other place," a teacher at Overbrook suggested. "It's hard for them to get to know each other when they live across the city."

THE LOSS OF COMMUNITY BONDS

Many magnet school parents described in depth and with deep emotion more troubling concerns. These issues relate to a sense of communities lost and of neighborhoods fragmented by aggressive busing efforts. This translates to a degree of anonymity and diminished familiarity and communication among neighbors; one mother of a young son at MaSAC observed that "communities that aren't communities anymore." Social ties and social institutions that formally bound these families around neighborhood schools and helped form geographical and functional communities (Coleman & Hoffer, 1987) have eroded due, at least in part, to desegregation policies. There is a perceptible loss of social capital (Coleman, 1987) that, for many parents, represents a troubling trade-off. Jacine Cody, the Head Start administrator who is also a parent at Greenwood and a strong proponent of magnet schools, nevertheless shares the concerns of many magnet parents, particularly African American parents, who are focused on issues related to neighborhoods, ethnic histories, and community fissures. Jacine observed:

> I grew up in a neighborhood school. Our teachers lived in the community. Our teachers would chastise us, we would go home and still get in trouble. I think our kids miss that. My son does not know anyone in our community and we have been there 17 years and he has been there all his life.

Althea Robinson, who is a teacher in the Cincinnati Public School District and a Greenwood parent, offered this account of a geographical community lost and a degree of social capital undercut by magnets:

> Now that we are forcing racial balance, we are taking kids out of their neighborhood, taking that family or that grouping away from them. When you teach in a neighborhood school, you have good rapport with the parents. They are up there all the time, bad or good; they can be up there. They may be up there ready to cut your throats, but at least they are there. You don't get that in alternative schools because of lack of transportation.

Shannelle Freeman, a MaSAC parent and a juvenile court counselor, described her own experiences in schools as places that represented mirror images of their neighborhoods. Her words convey a dark side of school choices that may disconnect neighborhood communities from their schools and dissipate neighborhood affiliations and ethnic bonds.

> My experience of growing up and going to a neighborhood school was as you walked, you picked up the whole neighborhood. . . . I don't even know my neighbors. Nobody knows their neighbors' children anymore. Once you start busing and everybody is going all over the place, you don't have a community anymore. You don't have the parents going together to the PTO meetings, sports, extracurricular activities. Because everybody—it is not a matter of not trusting your neighbor—it is a matter that everybody is busy trying to make it.

A parent of a MaSAC fifth-grader echoed this perspective of magnet schools as an engine for neighborhood fragmentation. Meisha Woods is a full-time college student majoring in African American Studies and the mother of three children:

> I think the initial intentions [of magnet schools] meant well, but I think overall it has not been the best thing because it is just breaking down too many ties that are too important to growth and nurturing. It has done more harm in the long run because nobody knows anybody anymore. You can see it on all levels.

Parents articulated similar sentiments regarding the magnet school program effects on a sense of geographical "community." This observation was offered by Ruby Fox, a nurse with a daughter at Greenwood, whose response to a question concerning familiarity with other families in her neighborhood provoked this immediate response: "You don't know who the parents are. . . . You never see the parents." Ruby then focused on the impact of the magnet school arrangement on the children who leave their neighborhood each morning and return each afternoon:

> I think the magnet system breaks down the neighborhood . . . because there is something to be said about the fact that you have pride in where you live. But if you take children to the other side of town, they are not going to know where they are at. There is no sacredness for anything because they don't care. They know they are going to leave in the afternoon.

These findings suggest an interesting paradox related to the debate around the notion of school as a community: What type of community promotes more robust home-school relationships: a geographic community or a value community? Our study suggests that some aspects of home-school relationships, such as parent involvement, can be sustained in value communities, particularly in magnet schools, while other aspects, such as interactions among parents and teacher communication with the home, are more effectively promoted in geographic communities. When parents choose magnet schools, especially those at a distance from their homes, they may trade a degree of parent and teacher interaction for a setting they believe is more conducive to their educational goals and beliefs. Parents in nonmagnet schools, especially nonintegrated ones, may exert more demands on the school than do magnet school parents, and in efforts to help the school improve, may view the school environment as more conflicted and less caring and supportive.

CONCLUSION

The results of the analyses, both quantitative and qualitative, suggest that magnet schools may be more successful in promoting school community than their nonmagnet counterparts through higher levels of parental involvement, school responsiveness, and a sense of shared values and purpose. Although the overall levels of school community and parental involvement are relatively low and "unremarkable," it is important to listen to the voices of magnet school parents who report a sense of belonging and responsiveness from their schools. Parents of children in magnet schools, despite geographical dispersion, tend to participate in school meetings, volunteer at school, and attend school events. They feel a sense of shared purpose with other parents who have chosen alternatives to the neighborhood schools. "Everybody has a common goal, a common mission."

Parents of children in magnet schools feel supported by school personnel; magnet schools are perceived to be responsive environments. Parents indicate that teachers really care about their children and they feel comfortable spending time at school. Parents report that teachers take the time to respond to their concerns.

To the extent that school community is viewed as a crucial aspect of a school's capacity to help all students achieve, these findings are important. "Within the context of systemic reform, capacity is the ability of the education system to help all students meet more challenging standards" (O'Day, Goertz, & Floden, 1995). Schools that can promote, support, and develop school community and home-school involvement should have increased capacity to help students achieve.

How can we assess the depth of the sense of school community in magnet schools? To what can we compare it? First, these conditions should be compared to the claims made by policymakers and advocates that controlled choice and magnet schools may serve as a critical link for promoting and enhancing school community (shared values, social cohesion, strong commitment, regular communication). Second, school community in magnet schools should be compared to schools with geographic communities. When we compare the nature and quality of community across these two types of schools, we conclude that magnet schools have a greater sense of shared mission than nonmagnet schools. If, however, we compare the levels of school community and involvement to the hopes and plans of policymakers and advocates, the assessment is not as positive. Granted, there is a sense of shared purpose and involvement in magnet schools; however, the nature and quality of involvement are somewhat thin and dry and not nearly as pervasive as predicted. Mary Driscoll (1995) reminds us that for schools to be communities, they must encompass both geographic and value-consistency aspects of community. The geographic side of community or the "territorial view . . . is rooted in a concept of interdependence, frequently exemplified by shared space" (p. 219). Parents who meet face-to-face regularly become more interdependent. The value-consistency element of community is not "characterized so much by shared space as by shared meanings" (p. 219).

This discussion raises important questions regarding magnet school arrangements that produce reconstituted communities, and the school district policies and practices that might serve to enhance or erode them. Our focus rests with the anonymity observed in magnet schools, and the loss of social capital in schools left behind in neighborhood communities "that aren't communities anymore."

NOTES

1. The first variable, parent involvement at school, is operationalized as involvement in seven areas (e.g., volunteering, attending meetings) (7 items, $\alpha = .79$). Parent influence measures the extent to which parents indicate they have influence in certain areas of school policy, such as setting school goals, grading policies, and the school budget (10 items, $\alpha = .91$). Parent-parent interactions asks parents about the extent to which they meet parents outside of school, such as in church and at sports activities (6 items, $\alpha = .81$). The amount of information the school provides to parents is measured by parent reports of the frequency with which they receive information about the school from a variety of sources, such as their child and school personnel (6 items, $\alpha = .78$). Teacher communication with parents measures the frequency of teacher communication with the home about educational activities (5 items, $\alpha = .91$). School climate measures the extent to which parents sense the school has a caring, supportive atmosphere that is welcoming to them (9 items, $\alpha = .82$). In addition, the analyses control for two variables that could account for differences between magnet and nonmagnet schools: (a) income level of the parents and (b) ethnicity.

To study home-school relationships in magnet and nonmagnet schools, we conducted discriminate analyses separately for the Cincinnati and the St. Louis data. Discriminate analysis is a multivariate procedure that distinguishes between groups of respondents based on a series of discriminating varibles. The goal of the analysis is to find a linear combination of variables that maximizes the differences between groups in the sample to determine which aspects of home-school relationships best distinguish between the two types of schools: magnet and nonmagnet.

2. The standardized discriminant function coefficients in Table 4.2 indicate the magnitude of each predictor variable in distinguishing between magnet and nonmagnet schools. A larger coefficient indicates these activities dominate the differentiation of magnet and nonmagnet schools. The sign of the coefficient, in conjunction with the sign of the group centroid, indicates the direction of the group differences. Thus, for example, the coefficient of $-.222$ on the variable 'amount of teacher communication with parents' in Cincinnati and the centroid for nonmagnet schools also being negative, $-.385$, suggest that nonmagnet school parents report there is more teacher communication with home than do magnet school parents.

CHAPTER 5

Magnet School Teachers and Their Workplace

Colorful posters advertising a wide array of school programs attract the attention of visitors to the magnet school office in St. Louis. The posters describe schools with curricular emphases on mathematics, fine arts, science, bilingual education, technology, and more. Nontraditional and diverse instructional approaches such as open classrooms, Paideia, and Montessori are also presented. This wide array of offerings is not unique to St. Louis or Cincinnati. A national study of over 3,000 magnet programs indicated that 37% offered a specific subject-matter focus, 27% used a unique instructional approach, 11% emphasized the arts, and 12% provided career-vocational education (Steel & Levine, 1994). What stands behind the names of the advertised specialized themes and approaches? What is the nature of teaching and learning in magnet schools? How do teachers describe their work in magnet schools?

Market theory suggests that a system of school choice should increase the innovation and diversity of curricular offerings and instructional strategies (Chubb & Moe, 1990; Goldring, Hawley, Saffold, & Smrekar, 1997; Witte, 1991). Under these assumptions, schools should be responsive to market pressures, namely parent interests and demands, by providing different types of schooling for different types of families.

In contrast, institutional theory predicts that the implementation of a system of choice in a public school system may constrain diversity and innovation. The institutional norms and cultures of both schools and districts can inhibit more change (Crowson, Boyd, & Mawhinney, 1996).

MARKETS, QUASI-MARKETS, AND PUBLIC MARKETS

Most school-choice plans are heavily rooted in market theory—a set of theoretical arguments based on fundamental economic assumptions about human and organizational behavior in the context of a marketplace. Market theory suggests that in this context, educational systems would offer and supply a much wider array of educational options to parents in response to their demands. Parent demands for diverse educational options would prevent the "sameness" of schools prevalent in the monopolistic public school system (Ball, 1993). Parents are presumed to be rational and ambitious consumers who will "demand" and shop around for the best school. They will choose a school that maximizes their own self-interests. It should be noted that there is nothing inherent in market theory that defines rational parent choices in terms of higher student academic achievement. Other preferences, such as religious values, safety, or educational philosophy, can define the market in which a parent wants to consume education.

In the marketplace, educational systems would supply numerous types of schools. Glatter, Woods, & Bagley (1997) suggest that supply may vary along seven dimensions: structure (e.g., charter school), curriculum, learning style, religion/philosophy, gender, specialization (i.e., gifted education), and age range. Diversification of supply would be attributed to educational personnel who would be intent on maximizing their own gains, for example, higher student enrollment that can offer them prestige, power, and influence in the system. Furthermore, to gain "market share," educators would not only seek to respond to demand, but would be compelled to create innovative choices for parents. Since there is no longer a guaranteed clientele, educators would respond to competitive pressures through innovation and change.

An alternative conception of a system of choice in the educational arena is a quasi-market (Woods, 1994). Le Grand (1991) specifies some of the key differences between markets and quasi-markets. On the supply side, unlike traditional markets, suppliers, namely schools, are not motivated by profit maximization. "Precisely what such enterprises will maximize, or can be expected to maximize, is unclear" (p. 126). On the demand side, consumer purchasing power is not exercised in terms of money; rather, it is manifested in terms of an earmarked budget. Thus, there are many intermediaries between the parent-consumer and the school-supplier (Le Grand, 1991). A quasi-market system "puts the emphasis more on creating a wide range of choices than on fostering competition between providers" (Glatter et al., 1997, p. 7).

Further delineation of the market concept applied to schools is the notion of a "public market" (Pierre, 1995). According to Pierre, a public market is distinguished from more traditional markets in three areas: (1) Entrance into the market is restricted by legislation and other public rules; (2) demand is based not on purchasing power but on public entitlements of rights to individuals; and (3) there is strong control of the public market. There are numerous regulations and processes that must be followed before an entity can be considered a school. Parents have a public entitlement and legal right to send their children to school; they do not need purchasing power to do so. Furthermore, once a school has entered the marketplace, there are numerous controls on that school, even in the case of charter schools and magnet schools.

We next turn to the institutional perspective, which in sharp contrast to market theory suggests that it is difficult to find diversification and innovation among public schools, even in a system of school choice.

INSTITUTIONAL PERSPECTIVES AND SCHOOL CHOICE

Institutional perspectives do not support widespread differentiation in a system of school choice. Institutional theory suggests that organizations are shaped by "the rules and belief systems as well as the relational networks that arise in the broader societal context of organizations" (Scott, 1983, p. 14). Institutional theory is an adaptive perspective of organizations; organizations change themselves to be congruent with their environments. Although a system of school choice may offer differentiation among schools, the strong institutional norms and cultures of school districts would not support widespread innovation and differences among magnet and nonmagnet schools. In fact, institutional theory predicts that there are strong beliefs about what constitutes a "real school," a school that matches the prevailing cultural beliefs about what schools should be (Goldring, 1996; Metz, 1990). Schools that are different from "real schools" may not appeal to parents, thus creating a system of homogenization rather than differentiation. Institutional theory suggests that individual organizations adapt in response to environmental norms, opportunities, and threats (Hannan & Freeman, 1989). Thus, organizations adapt themselves to be congruent with their environments, focusing on the "powerful institutional rules" held by public opinion and important constituents (Meyer & Rowan, 1977).

Scott (1995) suggests that institutional environments can be analyzed in terms of three pillars: regulatory, cognitive, and normative. The regulatory pillar emphasizes the "rule-setting, monitoring and sanctioning activities of institutions" (p. 35). Institutional environments are portrayed as "the elaboration of rules and requirements to which individual organizations must conform if they are to receive support and legitimacy" (Scott & Meyer, 1983, p. 149). This perspective suggests that schools will evolve to conform and reflect rules and codes. Schools will thrive, therefore, not because of "effectiveness and efficiency of market transactions but rather [because of] conformity with externally defined rules" (Scott, 1983, p. 125). School innovation would be difficult in the face of regulatory environments, where compliance is highly valued.

The cognitive pillar of a school's environment refers to the socially constructed, common understandings of organizational members about their environments. From an institutional perspective, then, schools must mirror or adhere to externally legitimated formal structures. "By designing a formal structure that adheres to the prescriptions of myths in the institutional environment, an organization demonstrates that it is acting on collectively valued purposes in a proper and adequate manner" (Scott, 1992, p. 31). School personnel will collectively interpret what they believe is valued by their environments and will try to conform to those beliefs. If there is a strong perception about what is considered a "good school," then more and more schools will try to emulate that standard perception.

The normative pillar of institutional environments specifies shared values and norms that guide organizational actors' adaptations. Schools conform to external norms, thus strengthening "long-run survival prospects" (Meyer & Rowan, 1977, p. 252; Zucker, 1987). These external norms are referred to as "myths" because they are widely held beliefs; they are believed to be true by a majority of individuals even though they are not objectively tested (Scott, 1992). School personnel may well believe that parents do not want a variety of types of schools, but rather hold broad consensus about features of an "ideal school" (Glatter et al., 1997).

From an institutional perspective, then, a system of school choice may not lead to innovation and diversification. Prevailing norms, cognitive interpretations, and regulations provide strong pulls to homogenize schools. Gewirtz, Ball, and Bowe (1995) note that "although the market is supposed to promote diversity of provision, it appears to have the opposite effect: being too distinctive in the marketplace is risky" (p. 143). District officials, teachers, and parents may ultimately have very traditional views about schools, not wanting to promote something that is different from accepted norms and customs. As Metz (1990) noted, "magnet schools, especially secondary schools, are subject to the pressures of tradition, despite their license to innovate" (p. 133).

INNOVATION AND DIFFERENTIATION
IN SCHOOLS OF CHOICE

We now turn to some of the empirical research that addresses innovation and differentiation in the provision of schools. As Ball (1993) states, "Why should it be assumed that all needs will be met in the market place, or even that more needs will be met; that is ultimately an empirical question" (p. 10). It is important to note that empirical research cannot adequately address market theory assumptions given that we do not have a market system within the public school arena. Consequently, much of the research relies on considerable inference, comparing public and private schools and other "market" experiments, such as vouchers.

A comprehensive study of three case studies in Great Britain following the implementation of educational marketplace reforms indicates that market reforms have not led to increased innovation (Glatter et al., 1997). In fact, in one of the three communities studied, greater uniformity was observed, rather than sharper differences.

In a related study of Grant-Maintained secondary schools—schools that can opt out of the local education authority and become autonomous institutions with direct funding from central government—Halpin, Power, and Fitz (1997) reported that "there can be little doubt that the autonomy of the kind afforded by opting out has no inevitable implications for the development of innovative practice" (p. 63). They continue: "Few of the schools in our sample have embarked upon significant curriculum reform" (p. 64). In a study of elementary schools in Great Britain, Hughes (1997) found that teachers were generally unaware of the parents' views about schools nor did the schools have any systematic way to discover what the parents views might be; consequently, teachers' practices were not influenced by parents' views. "In the few cases where this occurred, teachers appeared to be acting in what they perceived to be the best interest of the child, rather than responding to market forces" (p. 82).

In the United States, Sosniak and Ethington (1992) compared instructional practices and curricula in schools of choice and in other schools in a national sample of schools using the National Education Longitudinal Study of 1988. They found that the two types of schools, choice (e.g., alternatives, magnets) and nonchoice, use similar curricula and modes of instruction. "The extent to which schools are educationally different and the nature of the difference among schools are the same in typical non-choice schools as in our sample of public schools of choice" (p. 48). Similarly, review of the Alum Rock, California, voucher experiment found that instructional practices differed little among the mini-schools from which parents chose (Martin & Burke, 1990). Furthermore, Archbald (1988) found no significant differences in curricular and instructional variation between magnet and nonmagnet schools in the Milwaukee public school system.

In contrast to these studies, other research suggests that innovation has been stimulated by open enrollment and magnet school options in such urban centers as East Harlem, Cambridge, and Montclair (Carnegie Foundation, 1992). These findings are supported by Metz (1990) in her case studies that documented innovation in magnet schools in terms of distinctive curricula, unique student-teacher relationships, and diverse student bodies.

Two highly visible studies, one by Coleman and Hoffer (1987) and the second by Chubb and Moe (1990), also lend support to the notion that school choice can stimulate innovation in education. Both of these studies compared public and private schools in the High School and Beyond (HSB) national longitudinal data set. Chubb and Moe (1990) suggest that private schools are more effectively organized because of their relative autonomy from external bureaucratic constraints. Coleman and Hoffer (1987) found substantial differences in the curricula of public and private schools. For example, private school students are much more likely to take academic courses than are public school students.

A LOOK INSIDE: TEACHERS, CLASSROOMS, AND CONTEXTS

Teacher Backgrounds

One of the major criticisms of magnet schools is that a "creaming" effect occurs with respect to districtwide faculty assignment; that is, not only do magnets attract the "best" students, they also attract the best teachers in the district. In both St. Louis and Cincinnati, there are no significant differences between magnet and nonmagnet schools regarding the percent of teachers who are regular, full-time, certified faculty. On average, over 90% of all teachers are full-time, and have regular certification. There are, however, modest differences in the average educational levels of teachers in magnet and nonmagnet schools. Teachers in magnet schools are slightly more likely to hold master's degrees and other graduate degrees (55% in St. Louis) than are nonmagnet school teachers (48% in St. Louis). In addition, there are also significant differences in the ethnic background of magnet and nonmagnet school teachers. Magnet schools tend to have a larger percentage of teachers who are African American. For example, in Cincinnati, 27% of the teachers in magnet schools are African American, while 18% of the nonmagnet teachers are African American.

Although these data suggest that magnet schools are not creaming teachers in terms of status characteristics, there may be informal self-selection processes at work here. When we asked teachers why they chose a position at their present school, nonmagnet teachers indicated that they had no choice. Magnet teachers, in contrast, are significantly more likely than nonmagnet teachers to *choose* to teach in a particular school. These teachers report that they make their choices based on the theme or philosophy of the school, as well as the instructional programs offered to students. It may well be that motivational properties associated with parental choice, such as stronger school support, higher levels of satisfaction, and a greater sense of empowerment, also affect teachers' outlooks about their schools because magnet school teachers are much more likely to choose the school where they teach. In fact, Raywid (1989) argues that teachers who choose their schools will be more committed to them.

Curriculum and Instruction

Are there differences in the curriculum and instruction offered in magnet and nonmagnet schools? Our survey results suggest there are few substantial or remarkable differences. Teachers in both magnet and nonmagnet schools offer the large majority of instruction in self-contained classrooms. In some rare cases magnet schools include multigrade, multi-age classrooms or semi-departmental instruction.

Our findings do indicate, however, that teachers in magnet schools report less standardization in the curriculum. We asked teachers the extent to which they agreed or disagreed with such statements as "My curriculum relies heavily on textbooks, workbooks, and other published materials" and "A primary objective of our curriculum is to prepare students for standardized tests." Responses to the curricular standardization scale (5 items, α =.71) indicate that magnet school teachers, across St. Louis and Cincinnati, are significantly more likely to report a less standardized curriculum than nonmagnet teachers. Furthermore, magnet school teachers are more likely than nonmagnet school teachers to report that they have flexibility in their curriculum to meet the needs of individual students.

We then asked the teachers a series of questions regarding instructional strategies: the frequency of teachers' use of whole-class lecture; homogeneous ability grouping; peer-tutoring; seatwork; and individualized instruction. There are some indications that magnet school teachers are utilizing more varied instructional strategies. For example, magnet schools are less likely to group students homogeneously by ability and teachers implement less written seatwork than do nonmagnet teachers. There are no differences in other areas, such as the use of peer-tutoring and individualization.

We also wanted to know whether magnet school teachers utilize ancillary professional staff in such areas as music and art, and whether they provide extracurricular activities in support of the specialized themes. Again we find few substantial or significant differences between magnet and nonmagnet schools, although some differences between St. Louis and Cincinnati should be noted. In Cincinnati, for example, we found no differences between magnet and nonmagnet schools in the employment of full-time personnel in the ancillary areas of music and art. In most cases, both magnet and nonmagnet schools share personnel with other schools. We also found no differences in the extent to which magnet and nonmagnet schools offer various school-sponsored extracurricular activities, such as sports, instrumental music/band, chorus, dance, theater, visual arts, student clubs, and field trips. Additionally, there are no differences in the extent to which schools provide transportation to students to permit them to participate in these extracurricular activities. Finally, there are no differences between magnet and nonmagnet schools in the availability of various other special programs for students at the school, such as before/after school child care.

In St. Louis, all the integrated and nonintegrated nonmagnet schools employ full-time music teachers and full-time art teachers, while only a third of the magnet schools had full-time music teachers and full-time art teachers. In St. Louis we also found differences in the extent to which magnet and nonmagnet schools offer various school-sponsored extracurricular activities to students, such as sports, instrumental music/band, chorus, dance, theater, visual arts, clubs, and field trips. Magnet schools are less likely to offer sports programs and more likely to offer programs such as band or theater. Magnet schools, however, are far more likely to provide transportation for extracurricular activities (60% compared with 20% for integrated nonmagnets and 25% for nonintegrated nonmagnets).

The results suggest that school systems with magnet schools offer a wide array of choices in terms of both curricular themes and instructional strategies. However, beyond the advertised themes, there are few differences between magnet and nonmagnet schools in the way that instruction is generally organized and in the extent to which these schools provide different curricular offerings. The "sameness" of schooling predicted by institutional theory prevails in the St. Louis and Cincinnati school districts. Magnet and nonmagnet schools alike seem to offer traditional schooling, with few additions to bolster the special themes or unique magnet foci. Teachers report traditional instructional strategies dominated by whole-class instruction. How can we explain this traditional stance of all schools? Are market forces at work at all? Do schools have the requisite supports to implement and sustain innovation? We turn to this question in the next section.

Teachers' Work Context

Curricular innovation can be sustained only in an organizational context that values and supports such change. What is the context of work for teachers in magnet and nonmagnet schools? To address this question we rely on a conceptual framework developed by O'Day et al. (1995). They outline five dimensions of schooling, called organizational capacity, that are central to the work context of teachers and are necessary conditions for educational change. The five dimensions we examine are:

1. vision and leadership—leader articulation of and garnered support for a shared mission focused on teaching and learning;
2. collective commitment and cultural norm-shared responsibility for student learning and a culture of continual improvement;
3. knowledge or access to knowledge—information to implement the vision of reform;
4. organizational structures and management-structural and managerial changes to enhance success for all students; and
5. resources—instructional materials and human resources that enable students to attain higher standards.

In this section we focus on whether there are differences between magnet and nonmagnet teachers' perspectives of these five dimensions of teacher work context.* If magnet schools are going to be centers of innovation and change, certain aspects of the work context for teachers should be in place to support and sustain innovation. Magnet schools, like all schools, need the organizational capacity to promote school improvement and reap benefits that market forces may unleash.

Empirical research on these dimensions as they pertain to magnet schools in particular, or other schools of choice in general, is sparse. In terms of leadership, it is claimed that magnet schools need innovative, visionary leaders who are more entrepreneurial than more traditional school leaders (Crow, 1991). Blank (1986) used national surveys of comprehensive and magnet high schools and found some differences. Magnet school principals received higher leadership ratings than did nonmagnet high school principals in such areas as planning with staff, making core curriculum decisions, and staff selection. In contrast, comprehensive high school principals were more likely to be viewed as change agents, but there were no differences in the extent to which they encouraged instructional innovation.

Collective commitment and shared norms are crucial for school-improvement efforts and have been found to be more prevalent in schools of

---

*This section is co-authored with Charles Hausman and Katie Moirs (see Hausman, Goldring, & Moirs, 1997).

choice (Coleman & Hoffer, 1987). Smrekar (1996) reported that structures and processes embedded in magnet schools foster qualities of shared commitment and social cohesion.

Knowledge, or the information necessary to implement shared visions of change, is another important aspect of school change. Supporters of magnet schools note that magnet schools should have enhanced access to knowledge to implement specialized themes and unique instructional approaches (Hausman, Goldring, & Moirs, 1997). This knowledge should be available from two major sources: teachers with expertise and experience in the specialized theme of their schools and the development of networks with other specialized schools.

Resources and organizational structures that offer autonomy and reduced bureaucracy are central to implementing innovative curricula. Magnet schools need to garner resources to support the special instructional and curricular themes and to attract students of different races into schools in segregated neighborhoods (Rossell, 1990). Lee and Bryk (1989) and Chubb and Moe (1990) have made the case that only if schools are freed from the red tape and control of centralized school systems will choice and market strategies have any hope of making a difference.

Organizational Capacity

Our survey results indicate that teachers report moderate levels of organizational capacity in both magnet and nonmagnet schools (see Figure 5.1). In both school types, teachers described the vision and leadership and collective commitment and cultural norms as the most highly developed dimensions of organizational capacity. Teachers are most likely to agree that their principals articulate and garner support for a shared mission focused on teaching and learning, and that there is a shared responsibility for student learning and a culture of continual improvement in their schools.

Teachers in magnet and nonmagnet schools rated the other three dimensions of organizational capacity—knowledge or access to knowledge, organizational structures and management, and resources—less favorably. Teachers in both types of schools were less likely to agree that they have the knowledge and information necessary to implement the vision of reform or school improvement, that structural and managerial processes enhance success for all students, and that there are appropriate instructional materials and human resources to enable students to attain higher standards.

Not surprisingly, given the differential allocation of resources, nonmagnet teachers expressed the greatest displeasure with the availability of resources. Ironically, given their expertise around a specific theme,

Figure 5.1 Teacher Reports of Organizational Capacity

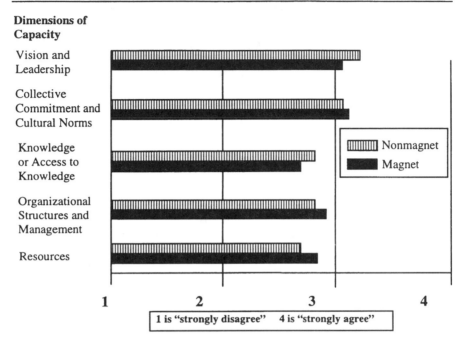

Dimensions of Capacity

Vision and Leadership

Collective Commitment and Cultural Norms

Knowledge or Access to Knowledge

Organizational Structures and Management

Resources

Nonmagnet

Magnet

1 is "strongly disagree"   4 is "strongly agree"

extensive networks with other similar magnet schools, and supporting coordinating agencies, the magnet school teachers ranked their knowledge or access to knowledge as the weakest aspect of organizational capacity.

To test for differences in overall organizational capacity and the specific dimensions accounting for such differences between magnet and nonmagnet schools, we utilized a MANCOVA with school enrollment and percent free/reduced-price lunch as covariates.[1] Significant differences in organizational capacity exist between magnet and nonmagnet schools.[2] Seven percent of the variance between magnets and nonmagnets can be accounted for by the five dimensions of organizational capacity operationalized in the model. Although this percentage may appear low, it is actually larger than the 5.9% variance accounted for in student achievement gains by the often cited model used by Chubb and Moe (1990) in *Politics Markets and America's Schools*. Analyses further indicated that two of the five dimensions of organizational capacity, organizational structures and management and resources, are discriminating between magnet and nonmagnet schools (see Table 5.1).[3]

Table 5.1 Structure Coefficients Derived from Discriminant Functional Analyses

Dimension of Organizational Capacity	Structure Coefficients
Vision and Leadership	.248
Collective Commitment and Cultural Norms	−.166
Knowledge or Access to Knowledge	.114
Organizational Structures and Management	−.370
Resources	−.554

Note: Loadings less than .30 are considered nonsignificant

In reference to the organizational structures and managerial practices at their schools, magnet school teachers indicate that they have more autonomy and influence in schoolwide decision making such as how the budget is spent. They also describe more freedom to be creative and fewer stifling rules and regulations.

Magnet school teachers also report more adequate instructional resources and assistance. Specifically, these teachers indicate greater access to professional support staff such as counselors and specialists, as well as additional clerical support. Magnet school teachers also describe more abundant instructional materials, as well as more current materials in good condition. Teachers' perceptions are supported by expenditure data. Data from St. Louis indicate that per-pupil expenditures on elementary students do vary, with magnet school students receiving more funding than students in traditional nonmagnet schools. Specifically, operating expenditure for magnet students is $4,377, while expenditure on students in integrated nonmagnets is $4,177. Since these schools have been in existence for over 10 years, this discrepancy cannot be explained by additional startup costs often necessary for magnet schools.

No differences were found between magnet and nonmagnet teachers' ratings of vision and leadership, collective commitment and norms, or access to knowledge at their schools. The same magnet school teachers who report greater influence, autonomy, and resources do not report stronger school vision and leadership than do nonmagnet school teachers. In addition, teachers at magnet schools express neither a greater commitment to student learning nor more knowledge about how to carry out visionary reform than do their nonmagnet school counterparts.

The results of this analysis are mixed and lend themselves to multiple interpretations. Both critics and supporters of magnet schools can find evidence to bolster their claims. Moreover, only two of the five dimensions—organizational structures and management, and resources—accounted for differences between magnet and nonmagnet schools; magnet school teachers report more positive organizational structures and management (i.e., greater autonomy and influence in the decision-making process) than their nonmagnet colleagues.

The precise cause of this increased report of teacher autonomy and influence should be explored. For example, does this enhanced autonomy and influence arise because magnet school teachers have specialized expertise around specific themes, are more committed as a result of choosing their schools, are members of a more tightly knit school community, or some other reason?

THE NATURE AND QUALITY OF
TEACHERS' WORKPLACE

The purpose of our case study analysis in this chapter is to explore the nature and quality of the workplace in magnet schools. To this end we asked: Is there something different (or better) about teaching in a magnet school? If so, compared to what? Would we know this is a magnet school if we walked in without that information? We were interested in teachers' perceptions of their schools in terms of climate, resources, and teacher collegiality. Our concerns center around the claims of market theorists who might predict a growth of diverse and innovative school environments in the context of controlled choice.

We begin by examining the advertised curricular offerings at the magnet schools in our study. First, a closer look at the two elementary magnet schools in Cincinnati, Mathematics and Science Academy of Cincinnati (MaSAC) and Greenwood Paideia. According to the Cincinnati Public School District (CPSD, 1993) magnet school handbook, the MaSAC elementary program "provides students with the opportunity to apply math and science to their everyday lives." The enriched math and science curriculum teaches students to understand numbers; grasp the meanings of addition, subtraction, multiplication, and division; compute and estimate in a variety of ways; and use the appropriate computation method for a given situation.

MaSAC enrolls 575 students in kindergarten through grade six, and is located in a working-class, predominantly white neighborhood on the western edge of the city. Approximately 83% of the students are bused to MaSAC from areas across the city. The school population is 51% African American and 49% white. Seventy percent of the students at MaSAC qualify for free lunch.

The Greenwood Paideia program is based on the philosophy that all students can learn; all students need and deserve the same high-quality education; all students must be challenged to perform to the best of their ability; and all genuine knowledge is active rather than passive. The district's magnet school handbook notes that the Paideia program "involves students in hands-on learning activities, higher level questioning and discussion, and cooperative learning." The program uses three methods of teaching and learning—didactic, coaching, and seminar.

As noted in Chapter 1, Greenwood Paideia enrolls 378 students in kindergarten through grade six and is located near an industrial park in a racially mixed, middle-class section of the city about 20 minutes from downtown Cincinnati. Approximately 95% of the students are bused to Greenwood from neighborhoods across the city. The student population is 52% African American and 48% white. Forty-five percent of the students at Greenwood qualify for free lunch.

"This Is Heaven"

While several teachers at these two schools were enthusiastic about their teaching and work life in magnet schools, all expressed greater joy simply to be out of neighborhood schools—places they described as among the bleakest and most dreadful of teaching environments. Teachers' sense of relief at having found a way out of neighborhood schools overwhelmed their descriptions of the teaching climate in magnets; this constant comparison provided the framework for considering the goodness and promise of magnets while recalling the despairing and distracting elements found in other schools. The "better than what" question was answered emphatically and unambiguously by teachers; magnets may offer less than they advertise, but they are safer and cleaner than neighborhood schools. They include a librarian in every magnet school and a computer in every classroom. The curricula may be largely standardized and traditional, but there is little fighting and no violence. The magnets provide enough books for an entire classroom of students and the desks, chairs, and windows are not broken.

Teachers' accounts of magnet school environments were often more compelling for what they said about the "other" public schools—the neighborhood schools left behind in the efforts to desegregate the St. Louis and Cincinnati school districts—than for what they revealed about the beneficiaries of these efforts. In stark and disquieting language, teachers described a public school system of haves and have-nots. All impressions of quality in magnets are measured against the inferior conditions they left behind in neighborhood schools. As one second-grade teacher noted when asked to describe the workplace environment at MaSAC, "It's a wonderful school to teach in compared to the inner city schools; it is like being in a demilitarized zone."

In Cincinnati, the MaSAC campus is considered by most of the teachers to be the main draw for parents. The school is located at the end of a quiet neighborhood street in a working-class community—a geography that provides a natural buffer against traffic, noise, and congestion. The school counselor noted that the well-manicured lawns, the thick groves of maple and shingle oak trees, and baseball fields encircling the MaSAC grounds around the school provide the perception "that it is more community-based and safer" than other, nonmagnet schools. "You don't find that downtown; it's all concrete."

Teachers described the conditions at MaSAC as "heaven" compared with teaching assignments in neighborhood schools. They made this assessment while acknowledging that their school lunch numbers are quite high (70%—second highest among magnets) and test scores quite low in reading (second lowest); MaSAC ranks in the middle of the magnets in math achievement scores. The teachers' recollections returned repeatedly to the notion that almost anything would be better than the "awful" conditions experienced elsewhere. Consider the following account from a fifth-grade teacher:

> I've been in bad situations. Last year I was in the church basement
> across the street from the [neighborhood] school. The kids were
> used to substitutes every day and I didn't have any interaction with
> teachers except when I was walking my kids to assemblies. This was in
> [a neighborhood] school that was built for 450 and there were 700
> kids. I was with two special education classes for behaviorally handi-
> capped children so the kids were always beating up on each other,
> banging on everything, breaking furniture. It was awful, really bad.
> Here, just the fact that I have a classroom with a chalk board. Last
> year all I had was a little portable thing on wheels. I guess my reasons
> for liking it here are a little crazy.

And this from a second-grade teacher:

> From where I came from, this feels like a country club school. I
> have materials. No one has pulled things off my wall. No one has
> called me a bitch, and I had second-graders in my last [neighbor-
> hood] school, mind you. I had roaches climbing over my walls,
> climbing on my plan book. Windows that were wood and came right
> off so a child could fall right out. No storage space. It was like a
> forgotten school. . . . I like it here.

Across town on the east side of Cincinnati, the principal at Greenwood Paideia, Miles Jackson, has established a strong reputation in the city for building a program "worth coming to." Four years ago, Jackson launched a recruitment drive to bring parents to his new magnet school. The efforts to sell the program took him to churches, community meetings, Head Start programs, neighborhood school assemblies, and news media offices. It paid off. Greenwood ranks at the top among magnets in both the math and reading achievement tests and has a waiting list of 600 students. Why do they come? Jackson argues that it is a "proven program" that offers safety, discipline, and excellence. In sum, he says, "it is a pleasant place to be." His assessment underscores the alternative: bleak, unsafe, and unruly schools that offer parents and their children a far less attractive educational environment. As Jackson argued, parents select his school due to the fact that the building is clean, unblemished by graffiti, and "because it is air conditioned; a lot of times air conditioning makes a big difference."

The teachers at Greenwood echoed their principal's claims. Their descriptions of climate and resources suggest little beyond the basic and expected: a school library, art and music classes, a handful of computers in the classroom (most of which are old and nearly obsolete Apple Macintosh models), occasional field trips to the zoo and to the local museum. These are not extraordinary state-of-the-art schools. Would we know this is a magnet school? It depends on whether we know what the alternative looks like. There is far less transiency here; students tend to stay at the school for the entire 6-year elementary school experience. Teachers enjoy readily available basic supplies—books, glue, paper, pencils, chalk, and erasers. And the teachers don't worry when they walk to their cars at the end of the day, as this fifth-grade teacher observed:

> We have people who came from schools where they were afraid to park their cars in the parking lot because they would come out at times and they would be smashed or they needed a guard to escort them out to the car at the end of the day. The doors were locked in the school where safety was a real factor. Those teachers have experienced the worst and now they are experiencing pretty much the best. I think they are real thankful.

The magnet schools have been extremely successful in attracting teachers based on the "better than the other" notion. As a fourth-grade teacher from Greenwood explained:

> In our district, the word was that the magnet schools seemed to have more things. They are the schools that more money was invested in.

So as a teacher, you would very much want to get into something like
that because the so-called neighborhood schools didn't get any of
the extras.

Nevertheless, most magnet school teachers are reluctant to accept the as-
sertion that magnets benefit from greater investments in education programs (or for that matter, from more involved parents). While there is clearly
a consensus around some of the physical or material differences between
magnets and nonmagnets, the teachers point out that most of the additional resources, such as math manipulatives, were made available at the
start of the magnet program and that spending on extras has long since
reached parity with the neighborhood schools. The principal at MaSAC,
Don Stockton, noted that although MaSAC is a math-science magnet, the
school's microscopes are generations old and outdated. There are no materials for the petri dishes, no centrifuges, and no incubators for science
experiments.

Likewise, few teachers could identify distinctive curricular differences
between their schools and others, despite the advertised curricular themes
at MaSAC and Greenwood. To be sure, while an emphasis on Paideia is
evidenced in the instructional strategies (lecture, coaching, questioning/
seminar) and role differentiation (teacher and coach) among the upper
primary grades at Greenwood, our daily classroom observations over the
course of a 4-week period suggested few distinctive instructional qualities
in the lower primary grades. When we asked about this, several Greenwood
teachers acknowledged that unless told, visitors wouldn't know the school
emphasized any particular pedagogy.

In the absence of extraordinary curricular differences, magnet teachers dismiss the notions of district favoritism and community elitism sometimes associated with their programs. Most redirected this critical viewpoint
and the attendant implications of privileging magnets over other schools to
a discussion of the institutional neglect of the neighborhood schools. The
reality of uneven and unequal conditions, however, tends to divide magnet
and nonmagnet teachers within the district. A second-grade teacher at
Greenwood observed:

> When you go to meetings and other teachers hear that you are at a
> magnet school, they are jealous of you. They are upset when they are
> working at one of the roughest schools that they don't have what you
> have. I tell them that I put in my time at the bad schools too and I
> did something that you can easily do. Instead of constantly complain-
> ing, I put in for a transfer and tried to make a change. I got that
> transfer and I got out.

A special education teacher defined the category of "definite" differences in physical appearance between Greenwood and the public school located just a block up the street from Greenwood. Fresh paint, new carpet, and air conditioning do make a difference, she argued, and teachers, parents, and students notice these things. These are the differences that mark magnet schools as separate and distinct from many of the neighborhood schools in Cincinnati. It is a difference that divides many people, she noted:

> I have a very good friend that teaches over there [the neighborhood school], but it is very difficult to talk to her about it. She gets so enraged because they have nothing and we have everything. Why is that? . . . We have land, grass. Normally these [neighborhood] schools are pavement pits.

Are these same differences in workplace qualities and characterizations evidenced in magnet and nonmagnets elsewhere? Let us take a closer look at the case studies in St. Louis, which focus on two magnet schools with identical academic programs: the Overbrook Basic Academy and the Viking Basic Academy.

Overbrook Basic Academy includes preschool through grade five. This magnet program emphasizes academic excellence through (1) a traditional basic instruction in reading, math, science, social studies, and language arts (students also participate in art, music, and physical education); (2) adherence to a "strict" discipline code; and (3) regular and consistent enforcement of a dress code. The Overbrook Basic Academy also emphasizes four fundamental principles: respect, responsibility, rights, and regular attendance. According to the Overbrook parent handbook, the curriculum is designed to promote academic development and "positive inter-personal behaviors and attitudes between the races."

As noted in Chapter 1, student enrollment at Overbrook is 253. The student population is 60% African American and 40% white. Over 90% of the students who attend Overbrook are bused in from different neighborhoods across the city and county. Sixty-four percent of the students at Overbrook qualify for free lunch.

Viking Basic Academy includes kindergarten through grade five. The academic program shares all of the elements of the basic program at Overbrook, including an emphasis on structure, discipline, and uniformity. Viking also offers enrichment and remediation in reading and mathematics through specialty magnet classes and the Chapter I program. In a unique partnership with the faculty at Harris-Stowe State College, which is located nearby, Viking provides computer and art instruction for all students.

Student enrollment at Viking is 298. The student population is 51%
African American, 45% white, and 4% "other." More than 90% of the students are bused from various neighborhoods across the city and county. Sixty-
eight percent of the students at Viking qualify for free lunch.

"We Are Different"

The portrait of a two-tiered public school system sketched by the magnet
school teachers in Cincinnati is replicated by teachers in St. Louis, who
describe their schools as places where children learn in environments that
are safe, orderly, and disciplined. St. Louis magnet school teachers enjoy
conditions that are markedly different from those they left in neighborhood schools. To begin with, there are the structural differences. The physical appearance of both schools is striking and impressive. The school build-
ings at Overbrook and Viking are nearly identical; both were built in the
1930s as part of the Roosevelt administration's Department of Public Works
projects. Both are three-story, brick, and blocky, with recently refurbished,
large double-hung windows that provide bright natural light for all the classrooms and school offices. The school corridors are wide and well lit with
glass and brass globe fixtures that have been restored to their original lus-
ter. Everywhere, the walls and ceilings appear freshly painted; the hard-
wood floors are buffed to a perfect sheen.

The schoolyards and their neighborhoods provide the only dramatic
distinctions between the two basic academies. There is a gritty, neo-urban
appearance to the hot asphalt yards at Viking, while eight miles south at
Overbrook, lush green lawns and mature red maples frame the cool, shady
entrance to the school building. Overbrook reflects the well-manicured
comfort of the more stable, middle-class neighborhood in which is nestled
protectively. Conversely, no buffer divides the Viking campus from the city
space that borders it: burned-out and abandoned low-rise public housing
side-by-side dilapidated rental properties.

Despite the real differences between Overbrook and Viking in physical location and landscaping, the magnets' collective qualities stand in stark
contrast to most of the neighborhood schools in St. Louis. Again, with prior
teaching experiences as a template to measure the nature and quality of
work life in their current magnet school assignments, teachers provided
richly detailed comparisons of essentially two different public school systems. When asked for an assessment of differences, a fifth-grade teacher at
Viking framed it this way:

> You would know the difference between this school and regular
> schools because the children are working here; they are busy doing
> something. The teachers are teaching. The halls are not cluttered

with kids yelling out. The building looks nice. There is no graffiti on the walls. The bathrooms are nice and clean. The school is orderly.

How would you describe your teaching experience in the neighborhood schools?

> The children would run up and down the halls. It was loud. You really were concerned about your safety there. There were numerous fights. They even beat up the principal one day. They waited for him to come out the door and they beat him up.

The repeated claims from teachers that "we are different" and "special" are striking not only in their consistency but also in the qualities identified that distinguish magnets from neighborhood schools. There were no references to the characteristics that many would predict related to distinctive curriculum, collegiality, or the "creaming off" of the most talented and credentialed educators. Even the markings of the basic academy—the academic core, discipline policy, and dress code—are considered incidental and ordinary. Instead, teachers pointed to the conditions of schooling that ought to be in place, that one would expect, in *every* school—order, discipline, safety, cleanliness. The school atmosphere emphasizes work, responsibilities, and expectations: Why are these elements considered so remarkable that teachers "feel blessed" to be in a magnet school? One teacher at Overbrook told us that "magnets schools are not better, it's just that they don't tolerate bizarre acting-out behavior" in students. The fact that teachers in these city school systems underscored over and over again the absence of violence and chaos speaks amply to darker and more distressing issues at work here. Why do teachers, as several reported to us in St. Louis, brag that their students "don't bring guns and don't bring knives, oh no." What is the context for such remarkable claims? Mel Forrest is a fourth-grade teacher at Overbrook and a veteran of 18 years in the St. Louis public schools. He summarized the situation this way:

> You are looking for things that we do differently. We don't do that much different. We really don't. We are a basic school. I think we basically do what a school ought to do, maybe what the others aren't doing.

"We Are Kind of on Edge"

The dedication, satisfaction, and sense of promise that are widely shared among faculty members at the magnet schools in Cincinnati and St. Louis show signs of slipping into dispirit and disillusionment as teachers feel increasing pressure to live up to media-crafted images of excellence against a backdrop of increasing violence and discord in the cities' schools. Magnet schools are armed with fewer resources and support than the public and advocates envision, and the perception of magnets as specialized, distinctive, and market-driven is certainly misconstrued and, perhaps, unfair. The extras allotted to magnets may be measured in 20-year-old math manipulatives and obsolete computer technology. Magnets may have more resources for art, music, and libraries, and these differences should not be discounted. But these are not private schools gift-wrapped in public school money.

Although somewhat less concrete and measurable than the differences, there are critical *similarities* between these magnet and nonmagnet schools. The common bond shared among all teachers rests with the uncomfortable and uncompromising realization of the complexity of the lives of children and their families. The stresses are related to issues of child abuse, hunger, and violence in the lives of the students. The instances occur in St. Louis and in Cincinnati, and they are central in the professional and personal lives of teachers. Far removed from the details of school-choice plans or racial desegregation, these are stories of survival, pain, and social isolation. These problems in the private lives of children and their families trigger troubling dilemmas for teachers. As one teacher in St. Louis said, "We are kind of on edge a lot." Consider the reflections of these teachers. First Joyce, a one-year "veteran" at Viking:

> I have learned so much. I thought teaching was getting in here and making sure that they learned what they needed to learn. . . . I found out a lot of things that these students are going through at home, like parents on drugs, child abuse cases, and you have to bring that into the class and kind of teach each student in a different way. Some of them need so much more attention; they are not getting it at home. You really start to feel for them because they are going through a lot of adult things and then they come to school and we tell them to be kids. They don't understand how to do both. This is the biggest thing that I've learned here is that they are people and have lives outside of here and it affects what we do in here.

Roberta taught in a tough North St. Louis school for 8 years before transferring to Viking, where she has taught since 1985:

> We are starting to get things that I have never experienced. . . . I have one little girl who saw three drive-by shootings this summer—nine years old. They were all three relatives at different times. The mother decided she didn't want her and the courts put her in a

group foster home. They don't want her because she is too old. Nobody wants her and she is a holy terror. She goes home on weekends to mom who does not want her and she goes to the group home during the week. Her court psychiatrist told me to stop knocking myself out about her because she is lost. . . . This is upsetting.

In Cincinnati, the two fifth-grade teachers at MaSAC, Jill and Paula, have each taught for 24 years; most of that time has been spent at the math-science magnet. They sat down together one morning at the school for an interview that went over one hour. The two teachers spent much of this time describing students they see each day and every year: students who are hungry, who lack coats in the winter, and who are regularly abused in their homes by family members and family friends. For years now, Jill and Paula have provided as discreetly as possible (to avoid embarrassing the children) cereal, bananas, and peanut butter to those students for whom Friday lunch is the last meal until Monday breakfast at school (provided as part of the federal government's free-lunch program). They started their secret food program after some residents near the school told them about children who, over the weekends, were going through garbage cans collecting food scraps. The teachers also noticed fourth- and fifth-graders collecting pieces of uneaten sandwiches and untouched fruit from discarded lunch platters in the cafeteria and carefully wrapping it in napkins to take home. Their observations are sobering and disturbing. Jill:

> We come with children in primary grades knowing more about sex and real violence than they do about normal everyday survival skills, like using the restroom or sitting down in a chair for a reasonable amount of time. There are children who have never been read to. They have no idea if you held up a blue crayon, what color that was.

And Paula:

> There are days when I spend at least 35 minutes just letting them get off of their chests what happened last night or over the weekend because we can't teach until they have the satisfaction of knowing that there is another way, it doesn't have to be that way. . . . They have seen sex; they have experienced sex. They have been raped. They know what guns are. They know drugs and a lot of alcohol abuse. Some of them know hunger. And they cry. We are not supposed to touch them, but how can you let a little kid cry and not touch them?

CONCLUSION

The challenges facing teachers in urban school districts are often overwhelming. The faces of poverty, fear, and abuse are visitors to classrooms everyday. Magnet schools, in and of themselves, cannot combat these realities. Our survey data and case studies suggest that, although magnet school teachers report some unique benefits of magnet schools, they are in fact describing the basic elements that should be available in all schools. Teachers in magnet schools have more resources, but they are by no means lavished with excess materials. Teachers in magnet schools implement a more flexible curricula, but they are not implementing widespread innovative instructional designs. Teachers in magnet schools have more autonomy and involvement in decision making, but these decisions are not geared toward implementing innovative curricula.

It does not seem that magnet schools have spurred a flurry of market activity. There is a sameness to all the urban schools in our districts, a sameness that is rooted in the poverty of the children. It may well be that strong institutional forces are at work that preclude magnet schools from becoming unique, too "good" and too different. Our hunch is, however, that neither the institutional lens nor the market lens provides the correct pair of glasses from which to view the magnet school predicament.

These disturbing realities of children's lives raise difficult and distressing dilemmas for teachers. The issues of poverty and abuse necessarily transcend discussions of curriculum, family-school communication, and teacher autonomy. These images require us to consider policies far beyond the minutiae of magnet school plans in a sharp turn toward more fundamental concerns regarding the immediate needs of children and their families. We examine the issues of social equity, community development, school reform, and school choice in the final chapter.

NOTES

1. Because the five dependent variables are significantly correlated, a MANCOVA, representing a more statistically sensitive means test, was used to test for significant differences in organizational capacity relative to school type (i.e., magnet versus nonmagnets).

Furthermore, since earlier studies indicated that magnet schools in this sample are characterized by larger student enrollments and enroll students of higher socioeconomic status than their nonmagnet counterparts, enrollment and percentage of students qualifying for free/reduced-price lunch were included as covariates in the analysis (Goldring & Hausman, 1996; Hausman & Goldring, 1996). These covariates would influence organizational capacity on many levels, especially resources. For example, schools are allotted funding per pupil. Similarly, low SES students often receive additional entitlements. Therefore, schools with higher enrollments and more low-income students would have larger budgets. Including these covariates removes from the unexplained variability and from the treatment effect any variability that is associated with the variability in the covariates.

One assumption needed for hypothesis testing in MANCOVA is the assumption that the dependent variables have a multivariate normal distribution. To this end, stem-and-leaf plots for each variable were drawn and indicated that the distributions were normal. Normal probability plots provided further support of normal distributions.

A second assumption required for hypothesis testing in MANCOVA is the assumption of homogeneity of variance. The significance levels for Bartlett-Box F tests for each individual dependent variable indicated that there was no reason to reject the hypotheses that the variances in the two groups are equal. These univariate tests are only the starting point for examining the equality of the covariance matrices. A second test that simultaneously assesses the variances and covariances is necessary. Box's M test, which is based on the determinants of the variance-covariance matrices in each cell as well as the pooled variance-covariance matrix, provides a multivariate test for the homogeneity of the matrices. Box's M=18.01 based on a Chi-Square with 15 df, p = .267 indicates that there is no reason to suspect the homogeneity-of-dispersion-matrices assumption.

As a final issue in interpreting the MANCOVA, Elliot and Barcikowski (1990) caution against using univariate tests as follow-up procedures to identify variables that may be contributing to multivariate significance. They contend that multivariate significance may be caused by a variety of different relationships; therefore, discriminant function analysis, which takes into account the relationships between the dependent variables and between the dependent and the independent variables, is utilized to determine the contributions of dependent variables to multivariate significance.

2. Significance was indicated by Pillai's trace = .07, F = 14.91 (p < .001). Pillai's trace was interpreted because it is the most robust and conservative of the multivariate statistics. In other words, the significance level is the most accurate when assumptions are violated.

3. The most common method for using the discriminant function for interpretation of group differences is inspection of the size of the discriminant weights. Structure coefficients are the correlations between independent variables and the vector of composite scores obtained when regression equations are applied to respondents' scores on independent variables. Structure coefficients indicate proportion of variable variance accounted for by the produced discriminant functions. Because they lack the shortcomings associated with both raw and standardized coefficients, they represent a more useful interpretation of the nature of the function(s) or the dimensions(s) on which groups are discriminated. As in factor analyses, they serve as loading on functions, and a coefficient of ± .3 is considered significant (Crocker & Algina, 1986).

CHAPTER 6

Rethinking Our Choices

We began this book with a broad view of magnet school systems in the United States and detailed descriptions of programs in St. Louis and Cincinnati—the cities selected for our in-depth study of magnet schools (see Chapter 1 and Chapter 2). In this chapter, we revisit a cluster of critical themes that we believe are fundamental to rethinking the design and implementation of these programs crafted for public school choice and racial desegregation. Our intentions are twofold: first, to confirm and to clarify the claims and criticisms associated with magnet schools based on what we know from this study; and second, to raise a cautionary flag for educators and policymakers invested in magnet programs to consider the value of intersecting public policies designed to promote community development within a context of choice and equity. We begin with a discussion of the aims of magnet schools: desegregation, parental choice, and educational innovation and improvement.

DESEGREGATION AND THE PROMISE OF MAGNET SCHOOLS

Without compromise and with scant public notice, both St. Louis and Cincinnati use magnets effectively to create racially balanced schools in their respective school districts. Although the issue of racial desegregation tends to be muted by more vocal claims among educators and parents regarding magnet program stability, excellence, and instructional innovation, the evidence clearly indicates that the court-ordered desegregation guidelines from which these magnet school programs originated have been efficiently and explicitly addressed; on average, African Americans comprise about 60% of magnet school enrollments in St. Louis and about 50% in Cincinnati, with white students making up the difference. It is important to note, however, that in St. Louis, where African American students comprise 78% of the school-age population, only 15% of the city's African American students are enrolled in city magnets. While almost 13,000 African American students attend suburban schools that are part of the St. Louis desegregation plan's interdistrict voluntary transfer program, the large proportion of African American students in the city means that a significant and disproportionate number of African American students who apply for admission to a magnet school are placed on a waiting list.

The Perceived Value of Racially Integrated Schools

Magnet school teachers in both cities described with insight and emotion the compelling rationale behind their school charter. Although some regard authentic racial understanding and integration as "beyond us" and belonging more appropriately to the values modeled in family life and in community arrangements, teachers expressed widespread regard for the racial balance represented in magnet classrooms and school corridors. Sarah Grant, a third-grade teacher from Greenwood Paideia, punctuated the point:

> I believe in integrated schools. I believe in as many kids together from as many different backgrounds as possible. I think that is the richest education the kids are getting when they are going to school with so many different cultures. I think that is a very important thing for all kids, kids from different socioeconomic backgrounds, too.

Teachers at Overbrook Academy in St. Louis voiced similar sentiments about the value of racially integrated schools and were equally impressed with the results of their racially balanced environments. While magnet schools are not a perfect solution to racially segregated neighborhoods— a prominent feature of residential life in St. Louis, as it is in numerous U.S. cities (Orfield et al., 1997)—many view the central aims of the desegregation plan and the strategy of using magnet schools as a viable and worthy enterprise. Bill Rogers, a 24-year veteran teacher at Overbrook, explained this viewpoint:

> You can look out the window . . . and see black and white children playing together, which is why we were invented, and on that level for the children, it works. Now, of course when they get on the buses and go back to separate neighborhoods, it is hard to stay friends for life, but that is a community problem; it is not something we can solve in the schools.

Charlie Allen, the gym teacher at MaSAC for 12 years, concurred:

> I wish all the neighborhoods were racially and economically integrated so children could grow up in a diverse culture because when they get out of school, they are going to have to deal with all kinds of other people, rich and poor, black and white. And that is what schools have to provide. Neighborhoods don't do that. So you go to an alternative and you wind up busing.

Many teachers spoke specifically to the value of children "exposed to other cultures," the importance of "learning that they are just the same as you and me," and the goal of "kids learning to get along better" across racial/ethnic groups. They observed with pride the pervasive patterns of children mixing across racial groups socially and academically—in the classroom and out on the playground.

The Cost of Integration

Most teachers were quick to point out that the racial integration in magnets comes with a cost; when school systems transport children so far away from their neighborhoods, the social distance between schools and families grows to reflect the geographical space that separates them. This point was made repeatedly (see Chapter 4). But the justification for these policies and the willingness to sacrifice a sense of community for a manifest commitment to integration are constant reminders to teachers of a collective goal tied to improved racial understanding. And although there is a sense of doing battle with influences beyond their control, there is an unwavering belief that promoting racially integrated schools is an important contribution to larger efforts. As first-grade teacher Shanika Taylor at Viking Academy in St. Louis noted:

> You need to learn the cultures of others. There are students who hear things at home and they never would know the difference. They believe that until they are around another race and then they discover that these people aren't so bad after all. It is that sort of thing that I think about when I think about doing away with the busing.

In a similar vein, sixth-grade teacher Bill Rogers at Overbrook lamented the cavalcade of buses—11 in all—that transport children for up to one hour away from school to their neighborhoods across St. Louis. Is it worth it?

> In a perfect world, I guess what they would have done is integrate the neighborhoods, then children could go to their neighborhood

schools. But I wouldn't know how to do that. Maybe if they could magnetize neighborhoods.

Still, other teachers are not as convinced as Bill Rogers that busing, even under voluntary conditions within a magnet system, is worth the costs. These teachers are more critical of what they perceive to be unaltered attitudes about race, social structures that discriminate against African American students, and behaviors that suggest that "nothing has changed" when it comes to improved racial understanding and trust. Many pointed to the expense, time, and safety of bus riders as central concerns. Other teachers pointed out that the bus schedules have eliminated after-school activities and shattered the kinds of positive social interactions and stable relationships that activities such as scouting and sports engender. All are convinced that magnet schools offer only a temporary, insufficient, and inconvenient mechanism for racial integration. Consider the perspectives of two teachers from St. Louis. First, Mrs. Settle, who is white and whose Viking Academy utilizes 14 buses and 4 taxicabs for transporting students across the city:

> I'm not sure busing is working. Unless you have blacks and whites living next to each other and getting used to lifestyles, you are not going to have any more communication than you do now. I think integration of neighborhoods is the only way we are going to get integration in the schools to work.

Ms. Alvins, who is African American and teaches at Overbrook Academy, was more pointed in her assessment, arguing that desegregation efforts unfairly and disproportionately disadvantage African American students and their families (Morris, 1997). This critical perspective, although far less common in the viewpoints collected here, is no less important:

> Until housing patterns can be changed and people live together, like you know your neighbor and I know mine, there is no such thing as [racial integration]. . . . I think we are worse off than we were before, particularly black children. Once their schools were eliminated and they were bused into other areas, their culture, their heritage, their history, it was ignored. It still is. Even here, we have to fight for it.

Parents: "It's Worth It"

When we asked parents to weigh the cost of busing against the value of racially integrated schools, most parents—African American and white— echoed the majority of teachers in a belief that the goal of integration is "worth it." Consider the observations made by Ruby Fox, who is white and from Greenwood Paideia in Cincinnati:

> I like the magnet program because it offers so much diversity. . . .
> There is such a diverse group of students. My kids are more tolerant
> of a lot of things that I don't think they would have been tolerant of
> had we lived in a neighborhood that was primarily black or primarily
> white. I feel like they have been exposed to all cultures, not like just
> a Catholic school.

The issues of racism and intolerance born out of ignorance and isolation seem to coalesce for most parents into a perspective that considers school integration at the elementary school level an important starting point—both practically and symbolically. Althea Robinson from Greenwood spoke to this point with force and candor:

> Let me tell you why I didn't think that much of my neighborhood
> school. With me being black, all your home base is if you are black or
> white, they are going to have all the majority of those people in it. I
> wanted my children to be among a multiculture of people. That is
> the way I was raised. I wanted my son to know about little white kids,
> Jewish kids, German kids, Indian kids—that is what kind of friends
> he has now. You find that you have to bump your kids out into the
> world. I love my black people dearly, but I also know that when you
> get out of school, you are dealing with multicultures.

Chontay Parks, a parent of two sons at Overbrook Academy in St. Louis, said she was proud to learn recently that the city high school from which she graduated 11 years ago is now racially integrated. To see this over-crowded, comprehensive high school transform itself from a predominantly African American school with high suspension rates to a magnet school with a high rate of academic success gave Mrs. Parks "a good feeling." As a resident of a predominantly African American section of St. Louis (North St. Louis), she is convinced that the social values represented in the mag-net school model are as vital as the academic opportunities. Echoing the views of other parents we interviewed, Mrs. Parks was unequivocal in her defense of busing as a vehicle for promoting racial balance.

> They get to mix with children of different cultures. They learn about
> different cultures. We live in the north city and [the magnet school]
> doesn't keep them so isolated. They get to learn and be around
> other people so in the workforce, they won't be so green and dumb-
> founded. I really like it.

Almost all the parents we talked to expressed some concern about enduring patterns of racial and social isolation in their cities and suggested that magnets are a way of ensuring that early on, children learn to view other youngsters of different ethnic and racial groups as "the same" as themselves. This heightened sensitivity to ethnic diversity among schoolchildren was referenced repeatedly by parents as a means of ensuring that, as one father from Overbrook put it, "people can get along" later in life.

If nothing else, this "exposure" to other children from different racial groups signals an element of the public school system of which parents and their children—selected as they are based on racial criteria—are a vital part. At the same time, it is important to underscore the muted emphasis on race evidenced in district rhetoric and in conversation with participants. Although responses were typically vocal and detailed, the issues of race and ethnicity were addressed only after we prompted and probed parents, school officials, and teachers; race regularly *followed* discussions focused on the general goodness of magnets, the safety and security of the students, and the satisfaction of the faculty. We suggest that in addition to racial balance and multicultural awareness, magnet schools represent another set of important values and profitable investments. These benefits are vested in the currency of parental choice bundled around a set of advertised educational offerings.

PARENTAL CHOICE

Under the mantle of enhanced parental choice, magnet schools offer an opportunity for students and their parents to enroll as volunteers rather than be assigned as residents of a particular neighborhood zone. As we noted in Chapter 3, the chance for parents to match their interests, preferences, and priorities with magnet school programs represents one of the most compelling features of this approach to choice. Our review of the literature suggests a set of basic assumptions around the exercise of choice. It is expected, for example, that enhanced choice creates communities of shared values that inspire the loyalty and commitment of parents and teachers (Chubb & Moe, 1990; Elmore, 1988; Erickson, 1982; Finn, 1990; McNeil, 1987; Metz, 1986, 1990; Raywid, 1988).

Choice and Equity

Our findings indicate other features of magnet school systems that are related to choice-making in contexts characterized by unequal resources unevenly distributed across parents of different social-class backgrounds. As we discussed in Chapter 3, we believe it is important to examine the resources available to all parents as they move through the choice-making processes that are a part of magnet school programs. Our intent is to highlight the ways in which parents' social networks provide access to the resources that are central for parents in managing and enhancing the educational choices offered by some school districts. Thus, rather than assume equal access to a market system replete with educational opportunities, we argue that the influence of cultural capital (Bourdieu & Passeron, 1990) on parents' abilities to exercise choice must be examined and made explicit.

These findings build on earlier ethnographic research that suggests that parents from higher social-class backgrounds arrive at school choice pivot points with greater resources than do lower-income parents (see Ball, 1993; Lareau, 1989). The greater material resources are derived from higher incomes, more extensive educations, and elevated occupational status (Lareau, 1989). These parents also tend to benefit from membership in social networks that provide stable and predictable channels of information and referral for questions critical for enhancing the educational experiences of children, including testing requirements, admissions policies, and special academic programs and scholarships (Smrekar, 1996).

British sociologist Stephen J. Ball (1990, 1993) argues that the market theories embraced by choice advocates belie a set of assumptions regarding the distribution of skills, competencies, and material resources (e.g., time, transportation, child care, etc.) that comprise a constellation of relevant factors in the context of choice. Without question, the process of negotiating the complex and obfuscated language of schooling is better mastered by those whose educational backgrounds and material resources provide access to the types of information and valued currency made so necessary in these educational institutions. Ball (1993) suggests that cultural capital pays dividends to parents in a number of ways, all of which are required in order to be active and strategic choosers:

> For example, knowledge of local schools, access to and the ability to read and decipher significant information, ability to engage with and decipher the "promotional" activities of schools, the ability to maximize choice by "working the system" (making multiple applications, applying for scholarships, etc.), and the ability to engage in activities involving positive presentation of self (e.g., when meeting key gatekeepers). (p. 13)

This work echoes Moore and Davenport's (1989) seminal study of public choice systems in four U.S. cities (New York, Chicago, Boston, and Philadelphia), which debunks the myth of equal access to these schools and underscores the centrality of cultural capital in the exercise of school choice. Similarly, our findings provide point and direction to issues of parents' abilities to understand the process of choosing. The concern rests with design problems and program flaws that privilege parents with greater material resources, especially in magnet programs that utilize a first-come, first-served admissions policy (rather than a lottery, as in St. Louis).

The Test of Equity

As parents in Cincinnati observed, only those families with reliable automobiles, chunks of discretionary time, and in some cases cellular telephones are able to gain entry to the most popular magnet programs under these admissions arrangements.

Besides admissions policies, far too little attention is paid to the differential effects of district information dissemination plans. For those parents who are unfamiliar with the language of schooling and are intimidated by "the messenger," targeted outreach designed to reach hard-to-contact parents should not be an option, it should be a requirement in all magnet systems. The source and quality of information should not constitute an obstacle for participation among a certain disenfranchised segment of the school population. We argue in Chapter 3 that these conditions provoke broad strategies that "tap into" the lines of trust and communication established by existing social networks and community-based organizations, including civic and volunteer organizations. Besides providing parent information centers (PICs), the information-dissemination plan should include outreach to the families who, due to economic circumstances, are among the most socially and residentially isolated. The key here is an effort that expands channels of communication and information exchange in an environment that is considered by participants to be trustworthy and reliable.

Still, as Ball (1993) notes, despite the best efforts of school districts dedicated to broad-based buy-in, some parents will "self-exclude" from the public choice system due to a belief that the arrangement does not "work for them" (p. 14). Parents who appear unwilling or unable to participate, or even ignorant of the options available in a magnet system, signify a further dimension to the sometimes discriminatory aspects of the culture of choice. Ball argues that "the system of choice presupposes a set of values which give primacy to comparison, mobility and long-term planning; it ignores those cultures which give primacy to the values of community and locality" (p. 14). We examine these values next.

COMMUNITY AND CHOICE

As noted earlier, one of the primary claims of choice advocates rests with the enhanced social cohesion, commitment, and sense of community engendered in a context of school choice. In Chapter 4, we explored the conditions in magnet and nonmagnet schools and found a somewhat more complicated and confounding story of school community. Certainly, magnet school parents perceive their schools to offer elements that are constitutive of community—a sense of caring and support, a perception of shared values and goals; these parents tend to be a bit more involved in school events than are nonmagnet parents.

Choosing Anonymity?

Our findings related to perceptions of community are muddled, however, by the actual low levels of involvement overall (confirmed by our survey and interview data among both parents and teachers). Moreover, the accounts recorded by the in-depth interviews with parents and teachers indicate little familiarity or face-to-face social interaction among parents or between teachers and parents. The geographical dispersion among magnet school families creates certain social distances that cannot be overcome by the "remade" or reconstituted community that may be miles and miles away from magnet families' neighborhoods. As the gym teacher at MaSAC noted, when children live a 45-minute bus ride away, parents don't have any transportation, and mom and dad both work, "it is a big problem." In the absence of any special outreach initiative or creative community-building strategy, this lack of "shared space" in a context of "shared meanings" (Driscoll, 1995, p. 219) diminishes the nature and quality of parental involvement and school community in the magnets, and renders a far less positive assessment of family-school interactions than some policymakers and choice advocates would promote.

Communities Fractured

Other concerns relevant to the character of community emerge from our study. These findings rest with the conditions of neighborhood communities that are left behind in the wake of magnet school movements. Many magnet school parents and teachers lamented the disconnections among neighbors—relationships that in the past were characterized by familiarity and interdependence. As one parent in Cincinnati observed in the aftermath of massive busing and magnet school promotion, "our communities aren't communities anymore." The loss of communal bonds provoked nostalgic reminders of formerly close-knit, predominantly African American communities in which neighborhood schools were the norm and where, as one magnet school parent in Cincinnati recalled, "as you walked to school, you picked up the whole neighborhood." Another parent in St. Louis stressed the belief that "people should be able to stay in their neighborhoods and feel comfortable that their kids are being educated." And Jean Kelly, a mother of a fourth-grader at Overbrook Academy, was blunt about it:

> You should have a neighborhood school and you should live around the school. You get to know the parents. It would be more of a little community thing. . . . I would keep the kids in their neighborhoods where they belong instead of busing them.

INNOVATION AND ACADEMIC DISTINCTIVENESS

Magnet schools are sold to the public based on the attractive idea (and marketing strategy) that they represent distinct curricular offerings not typically available at traditional neighborhood or zone schools. As we reported in Chapter 5, the findings from St. Louis and Cincinnati indicate that magnet schools are different from nonmagnets, but not necessarily in the ways that are advertised or detailed in district documents. The differences have far less to do with unique curriculum than with adequate resources.

"We Are Not That Different"

Magnets, on the whole, reflect what schools ought to offer, what they should promise. Teachers report that unlike in many nonmagnet schools, a magnet school teacher enjoys a supply of books for every student, enough pencils and paper supplies to last the school year, and a school climate that is safe, orderly, and focused on learning. As a teacher at Overbrook Academy in St. Louis observed, "We don't do that much different. . . . I think we basically do what a school ought to do, maybe what the others aren't doing." There are fewer of the distractions and disappointments that rob teachers of their morale and motivation, teachers say. To be simple about it, magnet schools are better than the alternative.

Blended with the reports on parents' reasons for choice and their understandings of what they have chosen (see Chapter 3), these findings have resonance and force. Parents, too, choose because of an unwavering faith in the goodness and promise of magnet schools in comparison to the alternative—the district's nonmagnet schools. These impulses are reflected in the top reasons parents list for choosing a magnet—academic reputation and style of teaching. As the interview data reveal, when probed for explanation and rationale, parents select for rather broad and unspecified reasons; for the most part, magnet school themes are irrelevant and function primarily as a proxy measure for "a good school" that is safe and not too far from home. Parents' understandings of the Paideia curriculum might be a

little fuzzy and vague, and they may mistakenly believe that the basic academies focus on math and science, but parents know enough to appreciate
the differences between magnets and nonmagnets. These magnet school
qualities translate into a "specialness" that all recognize. In one memorable
interview, a young mother struggled to describe in any specific way the distinctive qualities of the program at Viking Basic Academy. In a moment of
apparent exasperation with herself, she said with some finality, "The school
makes him feel important."

The Problem with Superiority

As common a sentiment as it is revealing, this young mother's viewpoint
may be unsettling for those who design magnet programs with the specific
intent of creating innovation in school systems known for their institutionalized and standardized features. But the undeniable reality may be more
difficult and much more troubling—that is, the apparent two-tiered arrangement embraced in magnet school systems. Mary Metz (1986) considers these
unequal arrangements the central irony in magnet school policies. As Metz
points out, in order to attract volunteers, magnet schools must be not only
distinctive, they must also offer a "practically superior" experience for students and their families (p. 208). Thus, the ultimate contradiction is culti-
vated through the rhetoric and the practice of magnets. In efforts to promote equality of educational opportunity in historically segregated systems,
magnet schools manifest superiority, and in doing so, violate this uniquely
American ideal of equal access to equal educational resources. These realities are not lost on either teachers or parents. Some expressed an openly
uncomfortable appreciation of the benefits they enjoy at the expense of
families who, for whatever reason, do not participate in the system of choice
and are relegated to what is, for many of the cities' students, an explicitly
inferior educational experience. Some may view this as the issue of the
"haves" and the "have-nots" that choice advocates often exploit and ignore.
Regardless, these realities force us to penetrate the veneer that has helped
slide the issue of magnet schools to the center of the policy table on the
naive and narrow assumption that these arrangements will solve the problems of equity and desegregation. We are reminded of these fundamental
truths by Van Brown, a father who is a teacher in a nonmagnet school in
Cincinnati and who has a son enrolled at Greenwood Paideia:

> I guess my biggest gripe is, why should magnets be deemed better if
> this is a public system? Why should anybody not want to go to the
> better schools? You are setting up a hierarchy. Somebody is losing
> out. If the schools aren't all equal, then why aren't they all equal?

WHAT'S OUR CHOICE?

The issue of equality is a stinging reminder of an ideal overwhelmed by multiple goals and competing values—desegregation, parental choice, and school improvement. As Metz (1986) reminds us, magnet school systems repudiate notions of equality to the extent that magnets reflect "superior" schools. These "better alternatives" are established in order to attract parents and students who would otherwise flee urban districts to enroll in private or suburban schools. We include "in pursuit of equity" in the subtitle of this book in order to amplify the significance of these competing interests at this particular time in the political history of school desegregation and school choice. In this final section, we explore these critical crossroads in education and social policy. First, we return to the data from our study sites in St. Louis and Cincinnati to examine social-class differences among the families in magnet and nonmagnet schools.

Social-class Isolation

As discussed in Chapter 1, the so-called creaming effect is one of the most enduring and pervasive claims against magnet schools. The concern rests with magnet program arrangements, such as selective admissions, limited (or no) transportation, and weak information dissemination, that exacerbate existing socioeconomic differences—and disadvantages—among parents. These types of magnet school policies are likely to produce sharp differences in the socioeconomic backgrounds of the students, with magnet schools enrolling a higher proportion of students from households with higher incomes, more education, and stable employment (Metz, 1990; Moore & Davenport, 1989).

  Our study of the systems in Cincinnati and St. Louis indicates that the impressive racial balance in magnets is not matched with socioeconomic balance between the magnet and nonmagnet schools. That is, our survey data clearly indicate that compared with nonmagnets, the magnet systems enroll students whose parents are of higher socioeconomic status with respect to income, education, and employment (see Chapter 3). In Cincinnati, which utilizes a first-come, first-served admissions policy in their magnet program, parents in magnets are twice as likely as nonmagnet parents to have a college degree and twice as likely to be employed. In terms of household income, only 24.9% of the parents in magnets report an income below $15,000 compared with 43.7% of the nonmagnet parents who report the same household income range (see Table 3.1). These differences between magnet and nonmagnet schools are consistent for all racial groups. Without question, these patterns reflect socioeconomic segregation in the Cincinnati and St. Louis public school systems.

The explanations for this pattern are explored in depth in Chapter 3, including the issue of parents' information networks and district outreach strategies that we believe contribute to the socioeconomic differentiation. The policy implications of this finding include district efforts that tap into existing community networks and that improve the quality of information available to those parents whose social networks may not be as broad or as accessible as the social networks available to higher-income families (Smrekar, 1996). But this notice and appreciation for class segregation does little to render these patterns any less pervasive or insidious. Perhaps less blatant than racial segregation, these concerns regarding social isolation have moved to the center in recent desegregation cases. In the Hartford, Connecticut, desegregation case (*Sheff v. O'Neill*), for example, the issue has overshadowed concerns regarding racial balance. (The poverty rate in Hartford is 63% and the city school system is essentially all minority—Latino and African American—with virtually all-white suburbs surrounding it.) Veteran school desegregation lawyer William L. Taylor emphasized the inseparability of race and class in an article in the *New York Times* entitled "Housing and Fear Upend Integration." Taylor observed: "I am more convinced than ever that if we're talking about providing really equal educational opportunity, then we have to confront the issue of racial and economic isolation" (Chira, 1993, section 4, p. 3).

The importance of addressing more fully and more swiftly the issues of class segregation is underscored by the most recent report by the Harvard Project on School Desegregation. In addition to providing new information on increasingly segregated school systems across the nation, the Harvard group (Orfield et al., 1997) writes that "the racial and ethnic segregation of African American and Latino students has produced a deepening isolation from middle class students and from successful schools" (p. 1). In general, racial segregation goes hand-in-hand with social-class isolation. The consequences are devastating for students and discouraging for those committed to educational equality. The Harvard report outlines some of these implications:

> School level educational achievement scores in many states and in the nation show a very strong relation between poverty concentrations and low achievement. This is because high poverty schools are unequal in many ways that affect educational outcomes. The students' parents are far less educated— a very powerful influence—and the child is much more likely to be living in a single parent home which is struggling with multiple problems. . . . The level of competition and peer group support for educational achievement are much

lower in high poverty schools. Such schools are viewed much more negatively in the community. (p. 17)

Harvard University researcher Gary Orfield (1993) concludes that a concentration of poverty dampens the spirits of students by diminishing their hope in and commitment to education. Middle-class youngsters bring certain values and cultural dispositions to school, Orfield argues. These include the values of self-discipline, the expectation of success, and a faith in the institution of schooling. These children are products of middle-class success. In contrast, poor students often arrive at school with the disadvantages apparent in many low-income households, including parents who are less well educated and who are distracted themselves by the discouraging and disabling effects of poverty. These children too embrace certain—and distinctly different—assumptions appropriate to their experiences.

In the context of St. Louis and Cincinnati, our study paints a different portrait than the one sketched by the Harvard researchers, but it is nonetheless a pernicious pattern; despite racially desegregated schools, the systems reflect, to some degree, a "creaming" of more socioeconomically advantaged parents and their children from neighborhood schools to magnet schools. Our scrutiny falls on the disparities in the socioeconomic composition of magnet versus nonmagnet schools. We argue that the differences in family income, parents' education levels, and employment status are troubling and should trigger efforts designed to expand opportunities for lower-income families to participate more broadly in the system of choice envisioned in the magnet program. In the next section, we turn our attention to an overlooked but enduring aspect of social isolation in our focus cities —intolerably high poverty rates.

Public Will, Personal Advantage

Today, many American cities and American suburbs reflect almost entirely different nations of people separated by class, ethnicity, and opportunity. Segregated white suburban schools are markedly less poor than the segregated city systems overcrowded with children of color; only 5% of the nation's segregated white schools face conditions of poverty among the children, as compared with 80% of the segregated African American and Latino schools (Orfield et al., 1997).

The school populations in the cities of St. Louis and Cincinnati reflect these national trends and mirror the more micro-level, sociodemographic patterns of many court-ordered, racially desegregated school systems in the United States (see Chapter 2). The latest figures indicate that Cincinnati's total district enrollment of approximately 51,000 is 66% African American, 32% white, and 2% other. Of the approximately 36,000 students enrolled in the St. Louis Public School District, 78% are African American, 20% are white, with 2% designated "other." As noted earlier, African Americans comprise about 55% of the magnet school enrollment in Cincinnati, and about 60% of the magnet enrollment in St. Louis.

But while these urban districts include school enrollments that are racially balanced, St. Louis and Cincinnati are among the poorest cities in the nation, and are significantly poorer than their suburban counterparts. St. Louis and Cincinnati rank 11th and 12th, respectively, in overall poverty rates (about 25%) among all U.S. cities with populations of 200,000 or more (U.S. Bureau of the Census, 1996). Even more distressing are the child poverty rates in these cities. In St. Louis, over 39% of the children are poor— almost twice the staggering national average of 21%. In Cincinnati, the child poverty rate rests at just over 37%. The proportion of students eligible for free lunch in each school district provides further evidence of this deep and enduring urban poverty. Again, as we noted earlier, while there are proportionately fewer poor students in the magnet schools, the overall poverty rate in these urban systems produces high rates of poverty across *all* schools. In Cincinnati, about 50% of all students in the magnets and about 80% of all students in the nonmagnet schools qualify for free lunch. In St. Louis, the rates are even higher; 71% of magnet school students and almost all—96%—of nonmagnet students qualify for free lunch.

As we noted in Chapter 5, the sense of hopelessness, despair, and disparity associated with concentrated poverty in these cities has a gripping effect on the parents, students, and teachers in all the public schools— magnet as well as nonmagnet. The irony here rests with the fact that despite the widespread, taken-for-granted appeal of magnet schools as the "better" alternative in these city systems, the teachers there report the same type and degree of family stresses. The repeated stories of survival, pain, and social isolation are as central to the teachers' lives as they are to the students and families who experience the violence, abuse, and hunger. The remark from a teacher in St. Louis who observed "We are kind of on edge a lot," is a call to consider the complexity of the lives of children and families who live in cities separate and apart from the comfort and safety of more affluent suburban communities.

In their book *Broken Promises*, Norton Grubb and Marvin Lazerson (1982) argue that although poverty has always been recognized as central to the conditions of children and families, policymakers have resisted targeting the structural inequalities that persist in schools, health care, employment, and housing. According to the authors, beyond the constant battles between conservatives and liberals regarding the limits of the welfare state, neither side "considers very deeply the economic basis of family life, though both understand that families are often at the mercy of economic forces" (p. 7).

Jonathan Kozol (1995) reminds us of the consequences of this policy choice in his vivid and poignant portrait of racial isolation and devastating poverty confronting the children and adults in the South Bronx, New York. In *Amazing Grace*, Kozol indicts Americans for their conscious neglect and collective devaluation of these children and their families; he argues that persistent and concentrated poverty is not accidental and that structural economic inequities require both a political and a theological response.

While some states and private foundations move forward to embrace the call for improving the lives of children and families in conjunction with the narrower goal of enhancing the effectiveness and efficiency of the delivery systems that serve them, action among policymakers at the federal and state levels offers little optimism. The cacophonous call to "end welfare as we know it" drowns out the rejoinder: "Replace it with what?" Response at the federal level appears limited to the devolution of the authority to manage (or cut) welfare benefits and to provide modest child care and employment training programs—a formula that is focused on the *systems* that serve children and families. As Lisbeth Schorr (1997) has observed, welfare *repeal* is not the same as welfare *reform*.

In a changing global economy that offers little financial security, the economic indicators for American families are even more bleak than the political ones. The continued loss of manufacturing jobs due to foreign competition, automation, and relocation to off-shore plants (which have lower labor costs) means a substantial loss in the types of jobs that offer good wages, adequate benefits, and steady employment. The growth sector for employment in the United States is primarily limited to service industries, which are subject to temporary or part-time arrangements, pay relatively low wages, and offer limited or no benefits (Zill & Nord, 1994). "Ending welfare as we know it" assumes that the labor market will provide employment opportunities that can support individuals at an hourly wage adequate to pay for housing, food, medical care, and child care, at least $8 per hour for a family of three (Jencks, 1994). The economic indicators suggest otherwise. The U.S. Bureau of the Census (1996) reports that median earnings for males *declined* between 1993 and 1994. Median household income was unchanged between 1993 and 1994 (in real terms), but was about $2,200 *less* than the 1989 prerecessionary median income. Census Bureau figures also indicate that the share of aggregate household income received by the top quintile was nearly 50% in 1994, continuing a pattern that has persisted since 1974 in which the share of aggregate household income received by the four lower quintiles has declined. These disparities in household income suggest a deepening and corrosive chasm between the "haves" and the "have-nots."

Perhaps as threatening as a wavering political will and an uncertain economy to children and families in need are the increasing signs of social and residential isolation, and racial segregation in America (see Orfield et al., 1997), as we have reported here. These conditions have led some scholars to suggest that the social ties that once connected Americans have violently eroded over the past decade in a convulsion of crass consumerism, elevated self-interest, and individualism (see Bellah, Madsen, Sullivan, Swidler, & Tipton, 1985; Elshtain, 1995; Lasch, 1995). According to this view, the perceived decline of communal associations, including such social institutions as families, churches, unions, and civic groups, has silenced the political discourse that enjoins individuals of different ethnic, class, and religious lines to common action. The spirit and activities of Americans, notes University of Chicago political scientist Jean Elshtain (1995), suggest a "culture of distrust" that displaces a sense of shared interests, collective commitments, and mutual interdependence:

> In an era of declining resources, resentments cluster around government-sponsored efforts that do not seem to solve the problems they were designed to solve. That is, citizens who pay most of the bills no longer see a benefit flowing from such programs to the society as a whole. Instead, they see a growing dependence on welfare, increased inner-city crime, an epidemic of out-of-wedlock births, and the like. They perceive, therefore, a pattern of redistribution through forms of assistance to people who do not seem to be as committed as they are to following the rules of the game by working hard and not expecting the government to shoulder their burdens. This is the perceived conviction, and it fuels popular anger and perplexity. (p. 4)

A public policy for children and families is tethered to this frayed line of public obligation by the sentiment that protects personal advantages in economic life. Kozol (1995) argues that these advantages are most prominent in our schools, health and juvenile justice systems, and housing arrangements. The issue of institutionalized disadvantage and disparity is elaborated by Mary Metz (1990), in a withering attack on those critics who threaten to derail the fast-track efforts designed to expand magnet schools. Characterizing magnet schools as sound policy measures pegged to choice, equity, and opportunity, Metz suggests that the indictments against magnets for alleged "creaming effects" are misplaced and unfair. The real outrage rests with the inequity long established and forever ignored—the abundant physical and human resources in suburban schools and the relative absence of those privileges in most city schools. While acknowledging that some magnet schools attract students who are slightly more "privileged" in terms of social-class backgrounds, Metz makes a compelling point about trade-offs in a context of private choices and personal advantages. Magnet schools keep parents inside a public school system and within the city limits—parents who would otherwise either flee to the suburbs or send their children off to private schools. (This battle rages on in Cincinnati, where only about 17% of the voters in the city have children enrolled in the Cincinnati public school system.) This lack of commitment to public education among families who have the means to abandon it, and most certainly will if attractive options are not made available within the public school system, provides a compelling rationale for magnet schools, despite the explicit tag of superiority that they engender. This is the irony that both sustains and threatens this desegregation policy. Metz (1990) concludes:

> U.S. education currently has a system of choice in education based on residence and the availability of private education for the well-to-do. The broad costs and benefits of magnet schools, and their specific effects on equity, must be calculated within the context of the reality of constant migration to apparently superior neighborhood and suburban schools by those whose skin color and financial resources give them the most options. (p. 143)

CONCLUSION

Against the backdrop of a cultural debate about public obligations and private choices, there is growing support for a public policy that moves schools beyond the traditional "development" needs of children to a deep involvement with the more entrenched issues of community revitalization. Without taking sides or silencing the debate between public responsibility and private morality, new, comprehensive, and long-term approaches are needed to rebuild social and economic capital in America's urban and rural communities. Empowerment Zones (EZs), for example, may signal a new era in government assistance for human development, community revitalization, and social service reform. Programs with strong community-level emphases, anchored to employment, job training, and private-public partnerships that are designed to stimulate economic activity and improve the quality of life (e.g., better housing, upgraded education, lower crime), should be a public-private partnership priority. Lisbeth Schorr (1997) argues in *Common Purpose* that the "enormous" potential of the EZ program design suggests that these initiatives "could serve as the vehicle for a massive infusion of investment to resurrect the nation's inner cities" (p. 359).

Children in neglected and isolated urban areas are vulnerable to the pathologies of rootlessness, hopelessness, and violence in the absence of a set of organizational and institutional affiliations (e.g., civic, recreational, religious, professional) that bind families in stable, predictable, and enduring social ties. The challenge rests with crafting public policies that reconstitute school-community linkages in ways that help promote school achievement, neighborhood and family stability, and economic revitalization (Wehlage, 1993).

The renewed emphasis on community revitalization addresses the need to improve the lives of children and families in conjunction with the narrower goal of enhancing the effectiveness and efficiency of the delivery systems that serve them. The issue of whether the fundamental "problem" is ending racial and social segregation, delivering more and better services, or rebuilding economic capital is not contested here, nor is the issue one of blame and responsibility. Initiatives that signal a convergence of complementary public policies designed to address public concerns—the well-being of children and their families—offer much hope. It is our choice.

Research Methodology

During the summer of 1993, the central administrative office in each of the participating school districts provided a directory of all public elementary schools in the district for the 1992–93 school year. Schools were chosen for the sample based on the following criteria: (1) the participating school included a fourth and a fifth grade and (2) the fourth grade was not the entry grade. These criteria were selected to increase the likelihood that each school would have a relatively substantial population of fifth-grade students who had been enrolled in the school for more than one year prior to the fall of 1993 (or the 1993–94 school year) and whose parents or guardians would therefore be relatively familiar with the school.

To reduce possible response bias, the initial sample frame was further screened, based on information provided by the central office, and schools were eliminated based on the following additional criteria:

1. Fourth- and fifth-grade classes assigned to the school were not actually attending that school in the 1992–93 or 1993–94 school year, for any reason, such as redistricting or renovation projects.
2. The school was a receiver of students reassigned for the same kinds of reasons, such as renovation or closure of their zoned school.
3. The school added or dropped a program within a 2-year period prior to the 1993–94 school year, resulting in a substantial change in the composition of the student body.

Out of 54 schools in the Cincinnati sample frame, 20 were selected for inclusion in the final study sample—10 magnet schools and 10 nonmagnet schools (see Table A.1). The final study sample of Cincinnati magnet schools was selected through a process of elimination by applying two exclusionary rules to the sample frame. First, magnets that were not full, or dedicated, were eliminated from the sample. (That is, schools-within-schools were excluded, as were magnets composed of a mixture of zoned and choice students.) As a result, 17 schools were eliminated. Next, of the 15 magnets

Table A.1 Sample Frame: Cincinnati

School Type	Sample Frame	Initial Sampling (Prior to Contacting Principals)	Final Sample
Magnet			
School-within-school	8		
Mixed	5		
Mixed School-within-school	4		
Full	15	10	10
TOTAL MAGNET	32	10	10
Nonmagnet	22	10	10
TOTAL	54	20	20

remaining, 5 were eliminated on the basis of information provided by the central office (during the late summer of 1993) that raised the possibility of significant response bias at these schools. Prior to the start of the 1993–94 school year, the district released the names of several schools, including 5 of the 15 full magnet schools in the sample frame, at which major programmatic changes were slated to occur during or after the 1993–94 school year. This announcement generated significant negative parental reaction to the proposed changes at these schools. Thus, these five schools were ruled out of the final sample, leaving ten magnets in the sample.

Also, after initially agreeing to participate, one of the 10 remaining magnets in the sample dropped out of the study during the school year. Thus, the final magnet sample contained nine schools, including two Montessori magnets, two Paideia magnets, three schools with a foreign language theme, one "fundamental academy" (emphasizing traditional curricular themes and instructional approaches), and one school having a mathematics and science curricular emphasis.

Twenty-two nonmagnet schools were included in the Cincinnati sample frame. Of these, 10 were selected for the final study sample by pair-matching them with the 10 selected magnet schools on the basis of the racial composition of the student body (using percent African American).

In St. Louis, the initial sample frame included 66 schools. Five were excluded because fourth and fifth graders were not actually in attendance, and four were excluded because they received large numbers of reassigned students, leaving an adjusted sample frame of 57 schools. Of these, 26 were selected for inclusion in the study (see Table A.2). This book focuses on

Table A.2 Sample Frame: St. Louis

School Type	Sample Frame	Initial Sample (Prior to Contacting Principals)	Final Sample
Magnet	10	10	10
Integrated Nonmagnet	36	10	8
Non-integrated Nonmagnet	11	8	8
TOTAL	57	28	26

students enrolled in the St. Louis Public School District and does not examine the suburban schools that enroll students from the city of St. Louis as part of the desegregation plan. For a detailed discussion of the experiences of African American students who choose to attend these predominantly white suburban schools, see Wells & Crain, 1997.

Magnet schools: All 10 elementary magnet schools in the St. Louis sample frame were selected. *Nonintegrated schools:* Eight of 36 nonintegrated schools were randomly selected for inclusion in the study. *Integrated schools:* Ten of the 11 integrated schools in the sample frame were initially selected by pair-matching them on racial balance (using total percent African American) with the 10 St. Louis magnet schools in the study sample. The principal of one of the schools selected declined to participate, citing the excessive paperwork that would be involved with both this project and the school's selection for participation in a mandatory statewide assessment program that was about to begin. The one remaining integrated nonmagnet school was then chosen to make up the sample.

However, after the first series of meetings with principals in early September 1993, two more schools had to be dropped from the sample. At one school, the fourth and fifth grades had been transferred out of the building because of a pending renovation project. The other school removed had changed its legal status from integrated nonmagnet to nonintegrated, effective with the 1993–94 school year. Therefore, eight integrated nonmagnet schools remained in the final study sample.

Data Collection

An anonymous questionnaire was distributed to all fifth-grade parents and to all nonadministrative certified staff in each school in the sample. Members of the research team visited each school and delivered questionnaires to a designated school contact person, who then distributed the parent questionnaires to the students through their fifth-grade homeroom teachers. Teacher questionnaires were distributed either in school mailboxes or during a faculty meeting.

The students were instructed to have their parents return the questionnaires in sealed envelopes to the school for subsequent pickup by the designated school contact person. Students were told that if 85% of their class returned the questionnaires, they would each receive a food coupon from McDonald's fast-food restaurant. Teachers returned their questionnaires in sealed envelopes directly to their school contact person. Members of the research team returned periodically to collect the returned questionnaires.

Schools with a low response rate were targeted for follow-up that included a second round of visits and calls to the school. Attention was given in the follow-up procedures to ensure that the racial composition of the parents responding to the questionnaires was equivalent to the racial balance of the school.

The response rate in Cincinnati was 62.1% ($N = 730$) for the parent questionnaire and 67.6% ($N = 417$) for the teacher questionnaire. The percentages of responses from African American and white parents from nonmagnet and magnet schools were equal. The response rate in St. Louis was 67.4% ($N = 953$) for parents and 70.6% ($N = 553$) for teachers.

Qualitative Multiple-Case Studies

This book also includes qualitative case studies of four magnet schools (one Paideia and one math-science magnet in St. Louis and two Basic Academy magnet schools in Cincinnati).

Mathematics and Science Academy of Cincinnati (MaSAC). According to the Cincinnati Public School District (CPSD) magnet school brochure, the MaSAC elementary program "provides students with the opportunity to apply math and science to their everyday lives." The enriched math and science curriculum teaches students to understand numbers; grasp the meanings of addition, subtraction, multiplication, and division; compute and estimate in a variety of ways; and use the appropriate computation method for a given situation.

MaSAC enrolls 575 students in kindergarten through grade six, and is located in a working-class, predominantly white neighborhood on the western edge of the city. Approximately 83% of the students are bused to MaSAC from areas across the city. The school population is 51% African American and 49% white. Seventy percent of the students at MaSAC qualify for free lunch.

Greenwood Paideia. The Paideia program is based on the philosophy that all students can learn; all students need and deserve the same high-quality education; all students must be challenged to perform to the best of their ability; and all genuine knowledge is active rather than passive. The district's magnet school brochure notes that the Paideia program "involves students in hands-on learning activities, higher level questioning and discussion, and cooperative learning." The program uses three methods of teaching and learning—didactic, coaching, and seminar.

Greenwood Paideia enrolls 378 students in kindergarten through grade six and is located near an industrial park in a racially mixed, middle-class section of the city about 20 minutes from downtown Cincinnati. Approximately 95% of the students are bused to Greenwood from neighborhoods across the city. The student population is 52% African American and 48% white. Forty-five percent of the students at Greenwood qualify for free lunch.

Overbrook Basic Academy. Overbrook includes preschool through grade five. This magnet program emphasizes academic excellence through (1) a traditional basic instruction in reading, math, science, social studies, and language arts (students also participate in art, music, and physical education); (2) adherence to a "strict" discipline code; and (3) regular and consistent enforcement of a dress code. The Overbrook Basic Academy also emphasizes four fundamental principles: respect, responsibility, rights, and regular attendance. According to the Overbrook parent handbook, the curriculum is designed to promote academic development and "positive inter-personal behaviors and attitudes between the races."

Student enrollment at Overbrook is 253. The student population is 60% African American and 40% white. Over 90% of the students who attend Overbrook are bused in from different neighborhoods across the city and county. Sixty-four percent of the students at Overbrook qualify for free lunch.

Viking Basic Academy. Viking includes kindergarten through grade five. The academic program shares all of the elements of the basic program at Overbrook, including an emphasis on structure, discipline, and uniformity. Viking also offers enrichment and remediation in reading and mathematics through specialty magnet classes and the Chapter I program. In a unique partnership with the faculty at Harris-Stowe State College, which is located nearby, Viking provides computer and art instruction for all students.

Student enrollment at Viking is 298. The student population is 51% African American, 45% white, and 4% "other." More than 90% of the students are bused from various neighborhoods across the city and county. Sixty-eight percent of the students at Viking qualify for free lunch.

The qualitative case studies focus on the context of school choice, the nature of school communities, and patterns of family-school interactions. Semi-structured interviews were conducted with the principal, counselor, and teachers (including a cross-section from both lower and upper primary levels) at each of the four sites. Interviews were also conducted with 12 to 14 sets of parents from each of three schools (two in Cincinnati and one in St. Louis). Parents were selected randomly from a stratified sample across race (two categories: African American and white) and social class (as indicated by eligibility for the federal free-lunch program). School records and parent data cards provided demographic information indicating parents' race, occupation, and city address. This information was used to select a sample of parents consistent with the socioeconomic and racial composition of the total population of school families.

Interviews with school staff were conducted at the school site; parents were interviewed in their homes. The interview sessions lasted an average of 90 minutes. All interviews were audiotaped, with participants' permission, and transcribed verbatim. In addition to interviews, an array of school documents (including brochures, enrollment applications, letters, newsletters, handbooks, and meeting minutes) was collected and analyzed.

Interview transcripts and document analyses were coded and summarized according to general descriptive categories using the constant comparative method (Goetz & LeCompte, 1984; LeCompte & Priessle, 1993). Converging pieces of information from interview transcripts were arranged according to broad themes and categories. Pattern coding (Fetterman, 1989; Miles & Huberman, 1984; Yin, 1989) was used to discern patterns of thought, action, and behavior among individuals and schools. To ensure anonymity, pseudonyms were used for schools and for individual participants in the study.

Variables Constructed from Survey Questionnaires

Chapter 4: Parent Survey

Parental Involvement at School (7 items, $\alpha = .79$)

How often do you or your spouse/partner do the following at this school?

Attend school meetings and parent-teacher conferences
Participate in fundraising events
Serve as a volunteer in the classroom
Go on field trips
Attend school performances, athletic events, socials, science or other fairs
Come to school when there is a problem or misunderstanding
Serve as a volunteer in the library, clinic, playground, or cafeteria

Parent Influence (10 items, $\alpha = .91$)

How much influence do parents in this school have in the following areas?

Hiring and firing school staff
Setting school goals
Setting school policies for discipline
How the school budget is spent
What is taught
Setting the school's grading policy
How money is raised
Ways the school and parents work together
Getting your child assigned to the teacher of your choice
How subjects are taught

Parent-Parent Interactions (6 items, α = .81)

How often do you or your spouse/partner interact with other parents from this school in the following ways?

> In church or at church activities
> At school meetings or through school organizations
> Through car pooling
> Through community sports programs or other non-school-related activities
> By living in the same neighborhood
> At work

School Information to Parents (6 items, α = .78)

How often do you receive information about the school and your child from the following?

> Your child's friends
> Contact with school personnel
> Television and newspapers
> Other children's parents
> Your friends and relatives
> Your child

Teacher Communication with Parents (5 items, α = .91)

How often does your child's teacher communicate with you about the following?

> Reading to your child or listening to your child read
> Playing games with your child related to his/her schoolwork
> Taking your child to a library, museum, or community event
> Tips on helping your child learn
> Asking your child about what he/she learns in school

School Climate (9 items, α = .82)

Please rate your agreement with each statement below:

> This school helps students achieve their best potential
> This school is a challenging place for my child
> This school is a safe place
> Teachers in this school really care about students and parents
> This school provides adequate opportunities for parents to be involved
> My child enjoys this school

The school's neighborhood is safe

The teaching strategies used at this school are innovative

I am uncomfortable spending time at my child's school

Chapter 4: Teacher Survey

Parent Involvement at School (7 items, α = .92)

How often do parents do the following at this school?

Attend school meetings and parent-teacher conferences

Participate in fund-raising events

Serve as volunteers in the classroom

Go on field trips

Attend school performances, athletic events, socials, science or other fairs

Come to school when there is a problem or misunderstanding

Serve as a volunteer in the library, clinic, playground, or cafeteria

Interactions with Parents (5 items, α = .65)

How often do you interact with parents from this school in the following ways?

In church or at church activities

At school meeting or through school organizations

Through community sports programs or other non-school-related events

By living in the same neighborhood

Through social contacts, informal telephone discussions, or chance meetings such as the supermarket

Communication about Home (5 items, α = .89)

How often do you communicate with parents about engaging in the following learning activities at home?

Reading to their child or listening to their child read

Playing educational games with their child related to his/her school-work

Taking their child to a library, museum, or community event

Talking with their child about what he/she learns in school

Helping their child with his/her homework

School Information to Parents (7 items, α = .71)

In general, how often do you contact parents about the following?

> Their child's placement in a particular instructional group
> Serving as a volunteer in your classroom
> Going on field trips with your class
> Coming to school when there is a problem or misunderstanding
> Serving as volunteer in the library, clinic, playground, or cafeteria
> Attending school meetings/parent-teacher conferences
> Participating in fund-raising events

Chapter 5: Teacher Survey

Curricular Standardization (5 items, α = .71)

Please indicate your level of agreement with the following statements about this school:

> My curriculum relies heavily on textbooks, workbooks, and other published materials
> My curriculum uses primarily short-answer tests to assess students' learning
> My curriculum focuses on state curriculum requirements
> A primary objective of our curriculum is to prepare students for standardized tests
> My curriculum was not designed to meet the needs of individual students

Vision and Leadership (13 items, α = .90)

Please rate your level of agreement with the following statements about this school:

> The principal is interested in innovative ideas
> My principal indicates an awareness of what goes on in my classroom
> My principal is highly visible around the school and makes many contacts with students and staff
> The principal does a poor job of getting resources for this school
> Extra efforts by staff are acknowledged and/or rewarded by my principal
> The principal deals effectively with pressures from outside the school
> At this school, teachers agree on the objectives we're trying to teach
> My principal's values and philosophy of education are similar to my own
> The guidelines in this school about what teachers are to emphasize in their teaching are not clear

The school has clear goals for student achievement

Most teachers at this school have values and philosophies of education similar to my own

Discussion about school goals is a regular part of faculty or in-service meetings

The principal of this school encourages teachers to talk with one another about instructional objectives

Collective Commitment and Cultural Norms (6 items, α = .61)

Please rate your level of agreement with the following statements about this school:

Teachers regularly share teaching ideas and materials

I think about transferring to another school

The teachers at this school like being here

Teachers in this school belong to a team that works well together

Teachers here are encouraged to turn to each other for help

Teachers in this school have high standards for all students

Knowledge or Access to Knowledge (9 items, α = .87)

Please rate your level of agreement with the following statements about this school:

When teachers are not doing a good job, the principal works with them to improve instruction

School faculty meetings help me do my job better

I receive informal evaluations of my teaching performance from other teachers

Performance-evaluation procedures in this school help teachers grow professionally

My principal is available when I need to see him/her

Other teachers encourage me to try out new ideas

Teachers receive the help they need form the principal when problems arise

The principal spends time in my classroom observing my teaching and provides me feedback

In-service training and staff-development programs in this school help teachers grow professionally

Organizational Structures and Management (21 items, α = .90)

Please indicate the level of teacher influence in the following areas:

Hiring and firing of school staff

Setting school goals

Setting school policies of discipline
How the school budget is spent
What is taught
Setting academic standards
Setting the school's grading policy
How money is raised
Ways the school and parents work together
How students are assigned to teachers
How subjects are taught
Determining the content of in-service programs
Selecting textbooks
Controlling the pullouts of their classrooms
Determining the amount of homework assigned

and, the level of agreement with the following statements:

I can take little action at this school until a superior approves it
I know what is expected of me but I also have the freedom to be creative
The rules and regulations at this school are rigid and inflexible
I am allowed to teach in my own style
I have a lot of discretion over what content I will cover in the classes I
    teach

Resources (7 items, α = . 79)

Please rate your level of agreement with the following statements about your work in this school:

I don't have all the textbooks, workbooks, or other instructional mate-
    rials I need
My instructional materials are outdated or otherwise poor in quality
I cannot get adequate clerical help when I need it
There are too few professional support staff, e.g., counselors, specialists
I cannot get the instructional resources I need for activities I have
    planned
I cannot get adequate information about my students' needs, abilities,
    or previous progress
I cannot get adequate assistance from teacher aides

Interview Guide for Parents

Biographical Data

> How long have you lived in this neighborhood?
> How many children in school? What ages?
> Are you employed? If so, what do you do?
> Are you married? single? significant other?
> Do you own or rent this home/apt.?
> How many years did you attend school?
> How do you spend any free time you might have? What do you like to do?
> Do you belong to any clubs, organizations, sports teams, etc.?
> Are you a member of a church?

Knowledge of the School

> What is the name of [your child's] teacher?
> Did you know anything about him/her before this year? reputation?
> Have you ever requested a teacher? If so, what did you know about the teacher? Where did you get the information?
> What is your child studying this year? What books does he/she read? What arithmetic do they know?
> What programs does the school offer for parents? programs for children?
> Did you attend parent-teacher conferences this year? Describe. What did you think? What did you find out?
> Do you visit school at any other times? Describe.
> What junior high, middle school will your child probably attend? What high school? Do you have any choices? preferences?

Meaning and Value of Schooling

> What do you want your children to gain from schooling? What is the most important outcome?

How much schooling do you think your children should have?

How far do you expect them to go in their schooling?

When you think about schooling, how does it line up in terms of other experiences?

What has influenced the way you think about schools? What has influenced the way you think about your role in your children's education?

Role of Parents in Schooling

What is your role in your children's education? Is it different from the teacher's role? How?

Do teachers expect things from you? What do they expect?

What do you expect from teachers?

Do you participate in your children's schooling?

How do you participate? Describe.

What are some things that keep you from participating the way you would like to?

Relations Between Families and School

How would you describe your relationships with school staff?

What do you think about the teachers?

What do you know about your child's teacher?

What does your child's teacher know about you?

How do you hear about things going on at school? Examples.

Have you ever contacted a teacher? Why? Has a teacher contacted you?

If you're concerned about something at school, what do you do? Describe.

Do you think your opinion counts?

What kinds of decisions should parents be involved in? Give an example.

Does this school belong to someone?

Conceptions of Parent Involvement

What does "parent involvement" mean to you?

How do schools tend to think about parent involvement?

Does anyone from the school talk to you about parent involvement? What does the school want you to do as a parent?

Social Networks

How often do you see other family members? Do they live nearby? Do you ever talk about school with them? What do they say?

Do you have any friends who work in schools? What do they do?

Do you ever talk about school with your neighbors or friends?

What do you think other families in the neighborhood think about this school?

Do you ever talk about the school or education with other people?

Do you know other school parents? When/where do you see other school parents?

Do you think other school families are people like yourself? (in terms of values, economic background)

How would you describe the parents at your child's school?

Is there a sense of community at the school? Describe?

Choice and Community

What are your expectations of this school? Are they any different than they would be at a public, or nonchoice school?

Why do you send your children to this school? How did you make the decision? Whom did you talk to about it? What things were important? How did you find out about the school?

What did you know about it when your child started school here? What do you know about it now?

How would you describe this school if you were advertising it (brochure, TV commercial)?

What about transportation to school?

How does it work if you want your child to come here?

Are you or your child expected to do anything more at this school because it is a magnet?

What is a magnet school? Why do we have them?

References

Almond, G. (1990). *A discipline divided: Schools and sects in political science.* Newbury Park, CA: Sage.

Archbald, D. (1988). *Magnet schools, voluntary desegregation, and public choice theory: Limits and possibilities in a big city school system.* Unpublished doctoral dissertation, School of Education, University of Wisconsin, Madison.

Archbald, D. (1996). Measuring school choice using indicators. *Educational Policy, 10*(1), 88–108.

Ball, S. J. (1990). Markets, inequality and urban schooling. *Urban Review, 22*(2), 85–100.

Ball, S. J. (1993). Education markets, choice and social class: The market as a class strategy in the UK and the USA. *British Journal of Sociology of Education, 14*(1), 3–19.

Bauch, P. (1989). Linking parents' reason for choice or involvement in inner-city Catholic high schools. *International Journal of Education, 15,* 311–322.

Bauch, P., & Goldring, E. (1995). Parent involvement and school responsiveness: Facilitating the home-school connection in schools of choice. *Educational Evaluation and Policy Analysis, 17*(1), 1–21.

Bauch, P., & Goldring, E. (1998). Parent-teacher participation in the context of school restructuring. *Peabody Journal of Education, 73,* 15–35.

Bauch, P., & Small, T. (1986, April). *Parents' reasons for school choice in four inner-city Catholic high schools: Their relationship to education, income, and ethnicity.* Paper presented at the annual meeting of the American Educational Research Association, San Francisco.

Becker, G. (1986). The economic approach to human behavior. In J. Elster (Ed.), *Rational choice* (pp. 108–122). New York: New York University Press.

Bellah, R., Madsen, R., Sullivan, W., Swidler, A., & Tipton, S. (1985). *Habits of the heart: individualism and commitment in American life.* Berkeley: University of California Press.

Bird, T., & Little, J. W. (1986). How schools organize the teaching occupation. *Elementary School Journal, 86,* 493–511.

Blank, R. (1986, April). *Principal leadership in urban high schools: Analysis of variation in leadership characteristics.* Paper presented at the annual meeting of the American Educational Research Association, San Francisco.

Blank, R., Levine, R., & Steel, L. (1996). After fifteen years: Magnet schools in urban education. In B. Fuller, R. Elmore, & G. Orfield (Eds.), *Who chooses? Who loses? Culture, institutions, and the unequal effects of school choice* (pp. 154–172). New York: Teachers College Press.

Board of Education, city of St. Louis. (1995, August). *Desegregation Report and Policy Statement.* St. Louis, MO: Author.

Bourdieu, P., & Passeron, J. C. (1990). *Reproduction.* London: Sage.

Bronfenbrenner, U., Moen, P., & Garbarino, J. (1984). Child, family, and community. In R. Parke (Ed.), *Review of child development and research, Vol. 7* (pp. 283–328). Chicago: University of Chicago Press.

Bryk, A., & Driscoll, M. (1988). *The high school as community: Contextual influences and consequences for students and teachers.* Madison: National Center for Effective Secondary Schools.

Bryk, A., Lee, V., & Smith, J. (1990). High school organization and its effects on teachers and students. In W. Clune & J. Witte (Eds.), *Choice and control in American education, Vol 1: The theory of choice and control in American education* (pp. 135–226). Bristol, PA: Falmer Press.

Bryk, A., Lee, V., & Holland P. B. (1993). *Catholic schools and the common good.* Cambridge, MA: Harvard University Press.

Carnegie Foundation for the Advancement of Teaching. (1992). *School choice.* Princeton, NJ: Author.

Chira, S. (1993, February 14). Housing and fear upend integration. *New York Times,* section 4, p. 3.

Chubb, J., & Moe, T. (1990). *Politics markets and America's schools.* Washington, DC: The Brookings Institution.

Cibulka, J. (1996). The reform and survival of American public schools: An institutional perspective. In R. Crowson, W. Boyd, & H. Mawhinney (Eds.), *The politics of education and the new institutionalism* (pp. 7–22). London: Falmer Press.

Cincinnati Public School District. (1993). *Alternative programs.* Cincinnati, OH: Author.

Clark, B. R. (1989). The distinctive high school, structural change, and the school reform movement. In S. Cohen and L. C. Solomon (Eds.), *From the campus: Perspectives on the school reform movement* (pp. 101–16). New York: Praeger.

Clewell, B. C., & Joy, M. F. (1990). *Choice in Montclair, New Jersey: A policy information paper.* Princeton, NJ: Educational Testing Service, Policy and Information Center.

Clinchy, E. (1989). Public school choice: Absolutely necessary, but not wholly sufficient. *Phi Delta Kappan, 71,* 289–294.

Cochran, M. (1990). *Extending families: The social networks of parents and their children.* New York: Cambridge University Press.

Cochran, M., & Brassard, J. (1979). Child development and personal social networks. *Child Development, 50,* 601–616.

Cochran, M., & Henderson, C., Jr., (1986). *Family matters: Evaluation of the parental empowerment program, a summary of a final report to the national institute of education.* Ithaca, NY: Cornell University.

Coleman, J. (1987). Families and schools. *Educational Researcher, 16*(6), 32–38.

Coleman, J. (1990). *Foundations of social theory.* Cambridge, MA: Belknap Press.

Coleman, J. S., & Hoffer, T. (1987). *Public and private high schools: The impact of communities.* New York: Basic Books.

Cookson, P. (1993). *School choice and the creation of community.* Paper presented at workshop, Theory and Practice in School Autonomy and Choice: Bringing the Community and the School Back, Tel Aviv University, Israel.

Cookson, P. (1994). *School choice: The struggle for the soul of American education.* New Haven: Yale University Press.

Coons, J., & Sugarman, S. (1978). *Education by choice.* Berkeley: University of California Press.

Crain, R. L., Heebner, A. L., & Si, Y. P. (1992). *The effectiveness of New York City's career magnet schools: An evaluation of ninth grade performance using an experimental design.* Berkeley: University of California, National Center for Research in Vocational Education.

Crocker, L. M., & Algina, J. (1986). *Introduction to classical and modern test theory.* Florida: Harcourt Brace Jovanovich.

Cross, R. (1994, April). *Do the influences of effective elementary schools endure?* Paper presented at the annual meeting of the American Educational Research Association, New Orleans.

Crow, G. (1991). *The principal in schools of choice: Middle manager, entrepreneur, and symbol manager.* Paper presented at the annual meeting of the American Educational Research Association, Chicago.

Crowson, R. L., Boyd, W. L., & Mawhinney, H. B. (Eds.). (1996). *The politics of education and the new institutionalism: Reinventing the American school.* Bristol, PA: Falmer Press.

DiMaggio, P. J., & Powell, W. W. (1991). Introduction. In W. W. Powell & P. J. DiMaggio (Eds.), *The new institutionalism in organizational analysis* (pp. 1–38). Chicago: University of Chicago Press.

Driscoll, M. E. (1991). *Schools of choice in the public sector: Student and parent clientele.* Paper presented at the annual meeting of the American Educational Research Association, Chicago.

Driscoll, M. E. (1995). Thinking like a fish: The implications of the image of school community for connections between parents and schools. In P. Cookson, Jr., & B. Schneider (Eds.), *Transforming schools* (pp. 209–236). New York: Garland.

Eaton, S., & Crutcher, E. (1996). Magnets, media and mirages. In G. Orfield & S. Eaton (Eds.), *Dismantling desegregation: The quiet reversal of Brown v. Board of Education* (pp. 265–289). New York: New Press.

Elliot, R., & Barcikowski, R. (1990, April). *Causes of multivariate significance in a multivariate analysis of variance.* Paper presented at the annual meeting of the Midwestern Educational Research Association, Chicago.

Elmore, R. F. (1988). Choice in public education. In W. L. Boyd & C. T. Kerchner (Eds.), *The politics of excellence and choice in education* (pp. 79–98). New York: Falmer Press.

Elshtain, J. (1995). *Democracy on trial.* New York: Basic Books.

Elster, J. (1986). *Rational choice.* New York: New York University Press.

Erickson, D. A. (1982). Disturbing evidence about the "one best system." In R. B. Everhart (Ed.), *The public school monopoly* (pp. 393–422). Cambridge, MA: Ballinger.

Fetterman, D. M. (1989). *Ethnography step by step.* Newbury Park, CA: Sage.

Finn, C. E. (1990). Why we need choice. In W. L. Boyd & H. J. Walberg (Eds.), *Choice in education* (pp. 3–20). Berkeley, CA: McCutchan.

Fossey, R. (1994). Open enrollment in Massachusetts: Why families choose. *Educational Evaluation and Policy Analysis, 16,* 320–334.

Friedman, M. (1955). The role of government in education. In R. Solo (Ed.), *Economics and the public interest* (pp. 123–144). New Brunswick, NJ: Rutgers University Press.

Gamoran, A. (1996). Student achievement in public magnet, public comprehensive, and private city high schools. *Educational Evaluation and Policy Analysis, 18*(1), 1–18.

Gewirtz, S., Ball, S., & Bowe, R. (1995). *Markets, choice and equity in education.* Philadelphia: Open University Press.

Glatter, R., Woods, P., & Bagley, C. (1997). Diversity, differentiation and hierarchy. In R. Glatter, P. Woods, & C. Bagley (Eds.), *Choice and diversity in schooling* (pp. 7–28). London: Routledge.

Glenn, C. (1993). *Providing parent information for public school choice in Massachusetts cities* (Report No. 4). Boston: Center on Families, Communities, Schools & Children's Learning.

Glenn, C., McLaughlin, K., & Salganik, L. (1993). *Parent information for school choice* (Report No. 19). Boston: Center on Families, Communities, Schools & Children's Learning.

Goetz, J. P., & LeCompte, M. D. (1984). *Ethnography and qualitative design in educational research.* San Diego: Academic Press.

Goldring, E. (1996). Environmental adaptation and selection: Where are the parents and the public? In R. L. Crowson, W. L. Boyd, & H. B. Mawhinney (Eds.), *The politics of education and the new institutionalism: Reinventing the American school* (pp. 43–53). Washington, DC: Falmer Press.

Goldring, E., & Hausman, C. S. (1996). *Reasons for parental choice of schools.* Paper presented at the annual meeting of the American Educational Research Association, New York.

Goldring, E., Hawley, W., Saffold, R., & Smrekar, C. (1997). Parental choice: Consequences for students, families, and schools. In R. Shapira & P. Cookson (Eds.), *Autonomy and choice in context: An international perspective* (pp. 353–388). London: Pergamon Press.

Goldring, E., & Shapira, R. (1993). Choice, empowerment and involvement: What satisfies parents? *Educational Evaluation and Policy Analysis, 15*(4), 396–409.

Grubb, W. N., & Lazerson, M. (1982). *Broken promises.* Chicago: University of Chicago Press.

Halpin, D., Power, S., & Fitz, J. (1997). Opting into the past? In R. Glatter, P. Woods, & C. Bagley (Eds.), *Choice and diversity in schooling* (pp. 59–70). London: Routledge.

Hannan, M. T., & Freeman, J. (1989). *Organizational ecology.* Cambridge: Harvard University Press.

Hausman, C., & Goldring, E. (1996). *Teachers' ratings of effective principal leadership: A comparison of magnet and nonmagnet schools.* Paper presented at the annual convention of University Council for Educational Administration, Louisville.

Hausman, C., Goldring, E., & Moirs, K. (1997, April). *Organizational capacity for school improvement: Teacher reports in magnet and nonmagnet schools.* Paper presented at annual meeting of the American Educational Research Association, Chicago.

Hirschman, A. O. (1970). *Exit, voice, and loyalty.* Cambridge: Harvard University Press.

Hughes, M. (1997). Schools' responsiveness to parents' views at key stage one. In R. Glatter, P. Woods, & C. Bagley (Eds.), *Choice & diversity in schooling: Perspectives and prospects* (pp. 71–85). New York: Routledge.

Jencks, C. (1994). *The homeless.* Cambridge: Harvard University Press.

Kozol, J. (1995). *Amazing grace.* New York: Crown.

Lareau, A. (1989). *Home advantage.* New York: Falmer Press.

Lasch, C. (1995). *The revolt of the elites and the betrayal of democracy.* New York: W. W. Norton.

LeCompte, M., & Priessle, J. (1993). *Ethnography and qualitative design in educational research.* San Diego: Academic Press.

Lee, V. E., & Bryk, A. (1989). A multilevel model of the social distribution of high school achievement. *Sociology of Education, 61,* 172–192.

Lee, V. E., Croninger, R. G., & Smith, J. B. (1994). Parental choice of schools and social stratification in education: The paradox of Detroit. *Educational Evaluation and Policy Analysis, 16,* 434–457.

Le Grand, J. (1991). Quasi-markets and social policy. *Economic Journal, 101,* 1256–1267.

Levine, R. (1997, April). *Research on magnet schools and the context of school choice.* Paper presented at the Citizens' Commission on Civil Rights Issues Forum: Magnet Schools and the Context of School Choice: Implications for Public Policy, Washington, DC.

Madden, N. (1993). Longitudinal effects of a restructuring program for inner-city elementary schools. *American Education Research Journal, 30*(1), 123–148.

Malen, B. (1994). The micropolitics of education: Mapping the multiple dimensions of power relations in school politics. In J. D. Scribner & D. H. Layton (Eds.), *The study of educational politics. 1994 yearbook of the Politics of Education Association* (pp. 147–168). Bristol, PA: Falmer Press.

March, J. (1986). Bounded rationality, ambiguity, and the engineering of choice. In J. Elster (Ed.), *Rational choice* (pp. 142–170). New York: New York University Press.

Martin, M., & Burke, D. (1990). What's best for children in the schools-of-choice movement? *Educational Policy, 4,* 73–91.

Martinez, V., Thomas, K., & Kemerer, F. (1994). Who chooses and why: A look at five school choice plans. *Phi Delta Kappan, 75*(9), 678–681.

Martinez, V., Thomas, K., & Kemerer, F. (1996). Public school choice in San Antonio: Who chooses and with what effects? In B. Fuller, R. Elmore, & G. Orfield (Eds.), *Who chooses? Who loses? Culture, institutions, and the unequal effects of school choice* (pp. 50–69). New York: Teachers College Press.

McNeil, L. (1987). Exit, voice, and community: Magnet teachers' response to standardization. *Educational Policy, 1,* 93–113.

Metz, M. (1986). *Different by design.* New York: Routledge.

Metz, M. (1990). Magnet schools in the reform of public schooling. In W. L. Boyd & H. J. Walberg (Eds.), *Choice in education* (pp. 123–147). Berkeley, CA: McCutchan.

Meyer, J. W., & Rowan, B. (1977). Institutionalized organizations: Formal structure as myth and ceremony. *American Journal of Sociology, 83,* 340–363.

Miles, M., & Huberman, A. (1984). *Qualitative data analysis.* Beverly Hills, CA: Sage.

Minnesota House of Representatives, Research Department. (1990). *Open enrollment study: Student and district participation, 1989–1990.* St. Paul: Author.

Moore, D., & Davenport, S. (1989). *The new improved sorting machine.* Chicago: Designs for Change.

Morris, J. (1997). *Voluntary desegregation in St. Louis, Missouri: Impact on partnerships among schools, African-American families, and communities.* Unpublished doctoral dissertation, Department of Educational Leadership, Vanderbilt University, Nashville, TN.

Newmann, F., & Oliver, D. (1968). Education and community. *Harvard Educational Review, 37,* 61–106.

O'Day, J., Goertz, M., & Floden, R. (1995). *Building capacity for educational reform.* New Brunswick, NJ: Rutgers University. (CPRE Policy Briefs, RB-18)

Office of Educational Research and Improvement, U.S. Department of Education (1992). *Getting started: How choice can renew your public schools.* Washington, DC: U.S. Government Printing Office.

Orfield, G. (1993). *The growth of segregation in American schools: Changing patterns of separation and poverty since 1968.* Alexandria, VA: National School Boards Association, Council of Urban Boards of Education.

Orfield, G., Bachmeier, M., James, D., & Eitle, T. (1997). *Deepening segregation in American public schools.* Cambridge, MA: Harvard Project on School Desegregation.

Ostrom, V., & Ostrom, E. (1971). Public choice: A different approach to the study of public administration. *Public Administration Review, 31,* 203–216.

Petronio, M. (1996, April). *Parents interact with school choice in Cambridge.* Paper presented at the annual meeting of the American Educational Research Association, New York.

Pierre, J. (1995). The marketization of the state: Citizens, consumers, and the emergence of the public market. In G. Peters & D. J. Savoie (Eds.), *Governance in a changing environment* (pp. 55–81). Montreal: Canadian Centre for Management Development.

Plank, S., Schiller, K., Schneider, B., & Coleman, J. (1992, October). *Choice in education: Some effects.* Paper prepared for the symposium Choice: What role in American Education, sponsored by the Economic Policy Institute, Washington, DC.

Raywid, M. (1988). Community and schools: A prolegomenon. *Teachers College Record, 90*(2), 197–209.

Raywid, M. (1989). The mounting case for schools of choice. In J. Nathan (Ed.), *Public schools by choice: Expanding opportunities for parents, students and educators.* St. Paul, MN: Institute for Learning and Teaching.

Rossell, C. H. (1990). *The carrot or the stick for school desegregation policy: Magnet schools or forced busing.* Philadelphia: Temple University Press.

Salganik, L., & Carver, R. (1992). *Information about schools of choice: Strategies for reaching families* (Report No. 5). Boston: Center on Families, Communities, Schools & Children's Learning.

Scherer, J. (1972). *Contemporary community: Sociological illusion or reality.* London: Tavistock.

Schorr, L. (1997). *Common purpose.* New York: Anchor.

Scott, W. R. (1983). Health care organizations in the 1980s: The convergence of public and professional control systems. In J. W. Meyer & W. R. School (Eds.), *Organizational environments* (pp. 157–172). Beverly Hills, CA: Sage.

Scott, W. R. (1992). *Organizations: Rational, natural and open systems.* Englewood Cliffs, NJ: Prentice-Hall.

Scott, W. R. (1995). *Institutions and organizations: Theory and research.* Newbury Park, CA: Sage.

Scott, W. R., & Meyer, J. W. (1983). The organization of societal sectors. In W. R. Scott & J. W. Meyer (Eds.), *Organizational environments: Ritual and rationality* (pp. 129–53). Beverly Hills, CA: Sage.

Smrekar, C. (1993). Building community: The influence of school organization and management. *Advances in research and theories in school management and educational policy* (pp. 1–24). Greenwich, CT: JAI Press.

Smrekar, C. (1996). *The impact of school choice and community: In the interest of families and schools.* Albany: State University of New York Press.

Sosniak, L. A., & Ethington, C. A. (1992). When public school choice is not academic: Findings from the National Education Longitudinal Study of 1988. *Educational Evaluation and Policy Analysis, 14,* 35–52.

Stanton-Salazar, R., & Dornbusch, S. (1995). Social capital and the reproduction of inequality: Information networks among Mexican-origin high school students. *Sociology of Education, 68,* 116–135.

Steel, L., & Eaton, M. (1996). *Reducing, eliminating, and preventing minority isolation in American schools: The impact of the magnet schools assistance program.* Report prepared for the Office of the Under Secretary, U.S. Department of Education, Washington, DC.

Steel, L., & Levine, R. (1994). *Educational innovation in multiracial context: The growth of magnet schools in American education.* Palo Alto, CA: American Institute for Research.

Steinberg, L. (1989). Communities of families and education. In W. Weston (Ed.), *Education and the American family* (pp. 138–168). New York: New York University Press.

Stevens, L. B. (1995, November). [Report regarding St. Louis Public Schools, Department of Justice Exhibit No. 90, *Liddell v. Board of Education,* E.D.MO. No. 72-100 (c) (6), March, 1996].

Taylor, W. (1996). *Magnet schools and the minority poor: Effective remedy or pyrrhic victory?* Paper presented on the annual meeting of the American Educational Research Association, New York.

Tenbusch, J. (1993, April). *Parent choice behavior under Minnesota's open enrollment program*. Paper presented at the annual meeting of the American Educational Research Association, Atlanta, GA.

Tversky, A., & Kahneman, D. (1986). The framing of decisions and the psychology of choice. In J. Elster (Ed.), *Rational choice* (pp. 121–141). New York: New York University Press.

U.S. Bureau of the Census. (1996). *How we're changing: Demographic state of the nation, 1996*. Washington, DC: U.S. Department of Commerce.

Useem, E. (1991). Student selection into course sequences in mathematics: The impact of parental involvement and school policies. *Journal of Research on Adolescence, 1*(3), 231–250.

Valente, E., Jr., Applebaum, M. I., Larus, D. M., & Faldowski, R. A. (1989). *Wake county public school system schools of choice program 1987–1989. Vol. 1—Main Document* (Research Memorandum No. 84). Chapel Hill, NC: University of North Carolina, L. L. Thurstone Psychometric Laboratory.

Voluntary Interdistrict Coordinating Council for the Settlement Agreement. (1994). *11th report to the US. District Court Eastern District of Missouri.* St. Louis: Author.

Wehlage, G. (1993). Social capital and the rebuilding of communities. In *Issues in restructuring schools* (pp. 3–5). Madison, WI: Center on Organization and Restructuring of Schools.

Wells, A., & Crain, R. (1997). *Stepping over the color line*. New Haven: Yale University Press.

Witte, J. F. (1991, November). *First year report: Milwaukee parental choice program.* Department of Political Science and the Robert M. La Follette Institute of Public Affairs, University of Wisconsin, Madison.

Witte, J. F. (1996). Who benefits from the Milwaukee choice program?. In B. Fuller, R. Elmore, & G. Orfield (Eds.), *Who chooses? Who loses? Culture, institutions, and the unequal effects of school choice* (pp. 25–49). New York: Teachers College Press.

Witte, J., Bailey, A., & Thorn, C. (1993). *Third year report: The Milwaukee parental choice program.* Madison: Wisconsin Department of Public Instruction.

Woods, P. A. (1994). School responses to the quasi-market. In J. M. Halstead (Ed.), *Parental choice and education* (pp. 124–138). London:. Kogan Page.

Yin, R. (1989). *Case study research.* Newbury Park, CA: Sage.

Yu, C. , & Taylor, W. (1997). *Difficult choices: Do magnet schools serve children in need?* Washington, DC: Citizens' Commission on Civil Rights.

Zill, N., & Nord, C. W. (1994). *Running in place: How American families are faring in a changing economy and an individualistic society.* Washington, DC: Child Trends.

Zucker, L. G. (1987). Institutional theories of organization. *American Review of Sociology, 13*, 443–464.

Index

NAMES

SUBJECTS

About the Authors

Ellen Goldring is Professor of Educational Leadership at Peabody College, Vanderbilt University. She received her doctorate in Educational Administration from The University of Chicago. Before coming to Vanderbilt, Dr. Goldring was Chair of the Educational Administration Program at Tel Aviv University, Israel. Dr. Goldring's research has focused on the organization and control of schools. She studies linkages between educational reform, principal leadership, and parental involvement, with particular emphasis on schools of choice. She has published widely about parental involvement and parent choice, school leadership, and organization theory in both the United States and internationally. She is co-author of Principals of Dynamic Schools (Newbury Park, CA: Corwin Press, 1993).

Claire Smrekar is an Associate Professor of Educational Leadership at Peabody College, Vanderbilt University. She received her doctorate in Educational Administration and Policy Analysis from Stanford University. Dr. Smrekar has conducted qualitative research studies related to the social context of education and the social organization of schools, with specific reference to family-school-community interactions in public, nonpublic, and choice schools. Her current research involves a study of the relationship between community development initiatives and the educational environments of at-risk students. She is the author of: The Impact of School Choice and Community: In the Interest of Families and Schools (Albany: State University of New York Press, 1996).